CW01476601

# Across the
# Borderline

## Eight great journeys

QUINTANA PRESS Ltd.

Peter Moss

First published in the United Kingdom in 2003
by Quintana Press Ltd.

Text copyright © Quintana Press Ltd.
Design copyright © Peter Moss
Photographs copyright © The Peter Moss Collection

**Across the Borderline**
Peter Moss
ISBN 0-9544650-0-8

Quintana Press Ltd
Brook Point
1412 High Road
Whetstone
London N20 9BF
Tel: 020 8952 4263
Fax: 020 8905 6474

peter.moss@virgin.net

*This book is for my friend Sean, who shares with me my love of travel, the films of Joel & Ethan Coen, and the music of XTC and The Clash. Let's trek again soon Sean; it's been far too long.*

All photographs in this publication have been taken by
Peter Moss . . . . even those of himself!

Across the
Borderline

Peter Moss

# Across the Borderline

## Eight great journeys

### ABOUT THE AUTHOR

**Peter Moss** was a rebellious and naughty child for whom travel became something of a necessity. After 10 years and more than 2,000 performances on the stand-up comedy circuit Peter now spends half the year travelling and the other half writing and talking about travelling … and football, and music, and religion, and much else besides. His articles and stories appear regularly in *The Independent on Sunday, The Guardian, The Jewish Chronicle, 4-4-2 Magazine* and assorted other publications. In a former life he was a scriptwriter, soccer coach, human rights lobbyist and occasional businessman. He lives in north London with his wife, two children, and twenty-five shares in Luton Town Football Club.

## Peter Moss

My heartfelt thanks go to Jan Shure for indulging my flights of fancy most Fridays in her travel pages. Thanks also to Triumph Press for all those colour copies, special thanks to Antonio and Dawn at Fratelli Café for your endless cappuccinos, and extra special thanks to Roger and Pino at La Brioche for even more endless cappuccinos, and for allowing me to show off my photos on your walls. To Karen and Mike at Mixed Images, huge thanks for your creative flair in putting this whole thing together. Mike, you're just an ageing old hippie. Keep walking barefoot around Hitchin in the depths of winter and they're sure to come and take you away. To Adina at the gym, thanks for stretching and soothing my aching muscles after each climb. Big thanks to Katie in Belize, Leanne in Bolivia, and Bazza in Morocco for making me laugh late into the night (Bazza, enough farting, right?) and really big thanks to Sean, Don, David and Greg for your company up, along and over countless ridges, passes and summits. To Susan, Lucy and Gideon, thanks for leaving me be to go on the road 26 weeks a year. I know you're in it for the duty free and the bizarre artefacts, but thanks anyway; you make so much possible for me. I need my space and you give it to me. To Andy Partridge and Robert Wyatt, genius songwriters both, I am eternally grateful for filling my head and my heart with such brilliant, beautiful music when I most needed it and pointing me in just the right direction at just the right times. Tom Waits and David Byrne, that applies to you too; Goran Bregovic, the concert in Bilbao made me cry like I never knew I could; and Joe Strummer and Warren Zevon, have you any idea how much you'll be missed? To Stewart Curtis, saxophonist extraordinaire, I offer you thanks for no other reason than you offered me thanks on your latest CD. Stewart, you're up there with Brecker, Marsalis and Coltrane and it's high time people knew. To Exodus Travel and Journey Latin America, I am endlessly impressed at the service you offer. You guys are so inventive and imaginative in creating pro-active travel for wandering souls like me. If Blair ran Britain as you run your organisations we'd all of us be Lords of the Universe. Bernard Kops, thank you for inspiring me to write all those years ago, and as for you, Roy Shuttleworth, what can I say? Had Humpty Dumpty had you to call on, he'd have needed neither the king's horses nor the king's men. You'd have put him back together again in no time. Thanks Roy…and special thanks, LB, for picking up the pieces I never laid before Roy. My brain was never better massaged. Finally, and perhaps most of all, I want to thank the people of each and every country I've visited, especially my guides, for allowing me access to the treasures that lie within. Thank you for letting me share your culture, your lands, and your lives. Each road travelled only makes me hungrier for more.

# Across the Borderline

## Acknowledgments

If I were Rob Fleming, the obsessive list-making hero in Nick Hornby's enduringly wonderful *High Fidelity*, I'd have listed every country I've been to. I'd have listed every town too…and river and mountain, hotel and restaurant, bar and bordello. What's more, I'd have graded them, say with five bagels and downwards, according to thrills, spills and the bizarre characters I'd run into along the way.

But I'm not a figment of anyone else's imagination. I'm just me, a middle-aged bloke who can't stop travelling. And as such I have not one single list of countries, either in writing or in my head, or…..oh, what the hell, yes I *do* have a list of countries visited, and yes, they *are* graded, and a good job too, as without the list or the grading I'd still be deciding which eight, of the fifty-eight countries I've visited, to focus on in this modest volume.

It was tough nonetheless settling on just the eight (seven, to be specific, plus one city). The easy part was wading through my portfolio of some 200 travel articles which I have been fortunate to have had published in various journals - primarily *The Independent on Sunday* and *The Jewish Chronicle* - these past five years. My files are well-ordered and everything is to hand. The tough part was figuring which would make the quantum leap from the regulation fifteen hundred words to something a little more meaty and book-worthy, because, frankly, I've found something on which to enthuse on pretty much all my travels. Eventually, and perhaps in deference to *Desert Island Discs* (which I still hope to be on one fine day), I got down to a final eight. But along the way there were casualties.

Ecuador and Spain came mighty close to making it into the book. Close, but not quite. So too Holland, my ancestral homeland, while Italy is a country of endless joy to me, notwithstanding its absence from this book. Belize, Bolivia, Cuba, Kenya, Israel, Morocco, Slovenia and New York City, on the other hand, *did* make it into the book. Not necessarily my absolute top eight destinations on the face of the planet - I'll say here and now my favourite place on Earth is the Galapagos archipelago - but certainly they represent eight truly exceptional journeys still warm in my memory to this very day.

Some of the journeys were physically arduous, others emotionally taxing, but all provided huge elements of the unexpected and the highly memorable. Some were just plain fun and each, in their own way, was hugely and positively life-enhancing…and that includes the episodes that challenged, and sometimes threatened, my very existence.

*Across The Borderline* first appeared as a track on Ry Cooder's "Get Rhythm" album back in '87. These days it appears - at least it should do - as a near-permanent entry in my passport. Am I complaining? Don't you believe it. I might tire of many things as I get older - taxes, parking tickets, David Beckham's apparent inability to settle on one hairstyle - but I'll never lose, to quote from a Joni Mitchell song, The Urge For Going.

peter.moss@virgin.net / December 2003

# *Foreword*

# Contents

# CLIMBING SLOVENIA

We strutted, we preened, we high-fived, we basked in our moment of victory... only to find, once the cloud lifted, that this wasn't even the summit. I don't think I ever felt so stupid, or crestfallen, as on that cold September morning high above Central Europe.

## Eight great journeys

I was 4-years old when I first opened an Atlas of the world. I started out with a junior version put out by Phillips - probably it was called Phillips Junior Atlas (but Mum, correct me if I'm wrong) - graduating to editions mapped, as it were, by Collins and, I seem to recall, the News Chronicle. I once got one for nothing, save for the thirty or forty tokens painstakingly torn off thirty or forty packs of Sugar Puffs and sent into Kelloggs. Special offers were *very* good in those days. I even had an Atlas put out by the Automobile Association, but the streets of London were never going to hold me.

Then came my barmitzvah. In among the dozens of pen and pencil sets, the obligatory leather briefcase, and the scores of cheques (some of which still haven't cleared, which tells you something about my dad's business associates), something big and green with a shiny gold spine stood out like a Rolex in a packet of sherbert dabs. The Readers Digest Atlas.

This, for me, was the defining moment of my young life. I pored over this wonderful tome, devouring every last map and statistic. I came to know each mountain and river, each desert and ocean, each graph and isobar, personally and intimately. I became a regular whiz at geography, naming any capital city my Uncle Albert would care to test me on. Geography became my best, perhaps my only, subject at school. I didn't even bother taking the 'O' Level. The official reason (a hopeless euphemism for forged letter) was tonsillitis. The official rumour was that Mossy was down the bowling alley hustling for florins. The real reason is that I figured the exam could not possibly offer me sufficient challenge. Pity. It might have doubled my tally of exam passes to two.

Never, between then and now - some 35 years later - would my bedroom, or latterly my office, be bereft of an Atlas, invariably on the floor, sometimes on a makeshift easel, and always open at my "country of the week". These days I own the gigantic and perfectly wonderful Times Atlas of The World. It cost me £125 - the best £125 I ever spent - and a few short months ago I had it open at Slovenia.

‹3

## With perfect timing...

With perfect timing, and definitely not as expected, given the opposite sides of the Atlantic from which we were arriving, my good friend Greg and I fetched up in Ljubljana within ten minutes of each other, he from New Jersey, me from London.

The weather was fine - warmer than expected, certainly T-shirt warm, and reasonably clear skies, though nowhere near enough blue to suggest we'd be in for anything approaching a rain-free week. We were greeted by Andrazj, one of the guides from Humanfish (the Slovenian equivalent of English adventure operators such as, say, Exodus or Explore), and whisked in his 4WD to the picture postcard lakeside town of Bled.

## CLIMBING SLOVENIA

We checked into the Grand Hotel Jadran - our base for the first night - and dumped our stuff quick as we could in our remarkably Soviet-style twin room (beds end-to-end lengthways; ideal for foot fetishists, not so ideal for buddy-buddy bedfellows, and good enough for me and Greg since we're neither, unless there's something he's not saying). It was mid-afternoon and we wanted to make the most of what was left of the day, travel fatigue notwithstanding.

And so, on the dot of 3, we set out for a brisk hike around the lake - so appealing and fairytale-like with its church-adorned island in the middle and hilltop castle across on the other side - and into the hills to seek out the Vintgar Gorge. We found it and it was sublime, stunning, with ice blue, clear blue, translucent blue waters flowing and tumbling down rivets and crevasses, along the river bed and towards the lake. It seemed - and this would be a recurring theme throughout the week - as though we had the place to ourselves. It truly was a lovely introduction to what is, as we would soon enough find out, a quite inspiring and thoroughly unspoiled country, one which seems to have found its first-world foot with commendable ease since going it alone not so very long ago from the old Yugoslavia.

We suppered on the terrace of a lakeside restaurant and checked out a sunset pierced and punctuated by spears of lightning and shafts of rapidly fading sun and rising moon. The view across the lake to the seemingly impregnable castle was just perfect, and never mind the drizzle that by now was falling into my mushroom soup and doing little, it must be said, to detract from either texture and taste, both of which were notable for their absence. Drizzle became rain, rain became downpour, and downpour became a dive back into our hotel, a dash upstairs, CNN on our TV, and an uncommonly early night.

*CB*

## And just what the hell is *'via ferata...'* ?

The weather has a mind of its own and today it's a mind in serious conflict. By turn grey-and-cloudy and almost-but-not-quite-sunny, we take it as it comes and commence to climb from the trail-head at Rudno Polje on the Pokljua Plateau up and into the mountains, specifically Mt. Triglav, at a shade under 10,000 ft. the highest peak in the Julian Alps, indeed in all of Slovenia, and a peak oft-used by serious climbers as a training ground for the higher reaches of the Himalayas, whose terrain and, as we are soon to find out, degree of difficulty is said to be startlingly similar.

The first hour or so is a shock to the system. It always is on a climb. It's not a physical fitness thing; you'd be an idiot to undertake a climb like Triglav without total confidence in your physical, *and* mental, condition, and Greg and I were, are, certainly in great shape. It's the adjustment, away from the flatlands of the big metropolis, to hauling yourself from a standing start straight up a one-in-three, soon-to-be one-in-two, gradient. Greg adjusts, as I see it, quicker than me. He's 31, I'm 51, I rest my case (if not my backpack).

After three-and-a-half hours on our feet we hit the 7,000 ft. mark. It's lunchtime, and for lunch read energy bar, the kind of absurdly chewy confection that reminds you just what a good living there is to be made in dentistry, and for some reason almost always involving either dark chocolate, peanut butter or...well, that's it, dark chocolate or peanut butter. I'm not keen on either. I eat three bars, dark chocolate *and* peanut butter. I find myself a bush and shit myself a roundabout. Local wildlife runs for cover. I consider serving *myself* with an environmental health notice.

The views, when the clouds deign to lift, are wonderful, a near-circular wall of granite enveloping us, with sheer drops to the valley a way below from the skimpily anorexic ledges and ridges that try their darndest to pass muster as a trail. And trail is a word, if there ever was one, in serious danger of breaching the Trades Description Act. If I tried to lay my two ballpoint pens side by side on the 'trail', one of them for sure would fall over the edge.

From the first refuge a short way further along the trail, we pushed on towards the overnight refuge, the one beneath - about a thousand feet beneath - the summit, the one called Triglavski dom, *dom* meaning refuge, refuge meaning somewhere to rest up before a stupidly treacherous climb becomes an even more stupidly treacherous attempt on the summit, the kind you have somehow, and with great selectivity it must be said, forgotten to mention to your insurance company, who have long regarded the most hazardous of your activities to be double-parking on Golders Green Road on a Friday afternoon.

This haul upto the 9,000 ft. mark is all but sheer. This is the start of the *via ferata* section. Via ferata, it turns out - and contrary, I might add, to my belief, for no apparently good reason, that it was something to do with fettuccini - means 'iron way', so called because this is the section where iron pitons, which have been hammered into the mountain wall by someone with extraordinarily good balance, are on hand to accommodate your tremulous hands as you edge your way across the flimsy ledges and up and down the vertiginous gulleys. In short, and in theory at least, it helps keep you on the mountain.

And on the really hairy sections where the pitons are connected by some sort of steel cable as a cunning handrail disguise, those climbers that are harnessed at last have something other than each other to which to be harnessed. Greg and I were not harnessed. We were not roped, cramponed, or indeed protected in any way. We were free-climbing, and to those of you who would ask the question: "Is that not a little irresponsible, not to say reckless?" I would reply something along the lines of:

"Well.......actually, yes". Still, I found out what *via ferata* is, and it's definitely nothing to do with Italian cuisine.

This section convinced me of what I always knew - the highest mountains are not necessarily the hardest. Kilimanjaro; 20,000 ft. and, at a push, one death per thousand climbers, and then more likely from extreme altitude sickness, or perhaps heart failure, rather than falling. Triglav; 10,000 ft. and - estimates vary wildly from tour operators who want your business, and seasoned Alpine climbers who know their business - somewhere between 20 and 80 deaths each year, per how ever many climbers take to the mountain (estimates vary far too wildly to quote figures).

The point is, this section was tougher, way, *way* tougher - and for tougher, read hazardous, and for hazardous, read downright dangerous - than anything I ever experienced five, ten, twelve thousand feet higher in the Atlas Mountains, on Kilimanjaro, or in the High Andes. We were never, whilst on the via ferata sections, more than the tiniest slip or slide away from tumbling down the mountain towards a brutal, bone-shattering demise, the kind that renders your climbers helmet somewhat...how shall I say...pointless. In fact, on Triglav you don't tumble down the mountain; you fall off.

And the danger was only heightened by the (by now) relentless drizzle that made the terrain more treacherous than is healthy even for the most sure-footed mountain goat. Greg - seemingly impervious to danger, and quite possibly the guy who does the stunts for Jackie Chan in films like *Fuck Me, I Just Fell Off a Mountain!* - was ahead of me (I know when to defer) and stopped every so often to photograph me and my apparently hilarious range of facial expressions, which I believe ran from gritty determination to steely resolve by way of scared shitless and Jesus-Christ-I-must-be-out-of-my-mind befuddlement and bemusement. Where others count sheep, I was counting life policies.

Still, we made it through that section, painstakingly and with no small skill, and with the most hazardous passage of this particular day's climbing behind us we glimpsed through furrowed brows the vague silhouette of an A-shaped structure up top of the ridge. Triglavski dom. Last stop, and only resting place, before, and a thousand or so feet below, the summit of Triglav. We quickened our stride, as one always does with the scent of a wood-burning fire and a pot to piss in descending from on high, and moments later we were removing boots, shedding backpacks, and supping from a hot tin cup.

The temperature had by now made its way from plus 15 to minus 5 in what seemed like moments and probably was. All the better, then, to be greeted by warmth, bonhomie, sandwiches, Turkish coffee, a cosy crowded dormitory, and the sound of *leider* songs from a contingent of enormous-thighed, bushy-moustached German climbers - serious climbers, climbers with faces hewn from chipped granite, and the ruddy complexion of those who get closer than most to the sun, and more often.

The ambience was wonderful, and all at once I realised just what it is I love most about being a bloke in the mountains. It's being in the convivial warmth that is generated by other blokes in the mountains after a hard and successful day's climbing. It's the kind of shared experience, and shared success, that scarcely needs to be verbalised. The fact you're at the refuge at all means you got there - and the absence of cable cars, funiculars and ski lifts means you got there the hard way. It's a good feeling, one of the best.

Greg is just great to climb with. Quiet and contemplative, he has the gift nonetheless of fielding and following up one of my randomly quoted passages from *This is Spinal Tap* or *Life of Brian* with consummate ease, and at considerable altitude. Many is the hour that passed merrily by with large chunks of the surreal and the sublime volleying between us. I'd say: "He's not the Messiah, he's a very naughty boy", he'd say: "But apart from that, what did the Romans ever do for us?" and...well...it doesn't really work if you haven't seen the film.

## CLIMBING SLOVENIA

At three inches taller and 20 years younger Greg moves up and down mountains rather quicker than me, and I'm no slouch. But we soon found a pace that suited the both of us, and if this meant Greg slowing a little more than he was used to, then for that I am truly grateful.

This had been a great first day. It could not have been tougher - it transcended the word 'challenging' and crossed the adjective divide towards 'hazardous' - and I guess we should be grateful for the incredibly dense cloud cover that prevented us, over long stretches, from having any kind of meaningful view. Because, frankly, during those last couple of hours inching and edging up to the refuge, I'd say we were best off not seeing what was up, or down, ahead of us, the deadly drop that awaited lest we get the tiniest bit careless, or nervous, or just plain unlucky, and hurtle down into the abyss.

When we set out at breakfast time from Rudno Polje, in late summer temperatures and with towering pines all around us, little did we know how, by the day's end, we'd be counting ourselves lucky to still be in one piece. And how much more satisfying to do this without a guide - just the two of us, a modest, but perfectly acceptable, knowledge of map-reading, and the wind in the right direction.

And the bonus - and what a bonus it was - the sound and sight of hairy great Germans rocking and swaying to the rhythm of their own drinking songs in a scene that recalled Max, Leo and the psychotic Franz Liebkind singing paeans to the Fuhrer in that well-known entertainment about Springtime for Hitler. What a great day.

And to make it greater still, we're advised by other climbers that of the dozen-and-more different routes up the mountain, we'd taken the sharpest and hardest, with all its contouring up and around the slopes and scrambling along summit ridges, accompanied by no small amount of holding on for dear life. Just can't get that Paul Simon tune out of my head. What's it called now? "Love Me Like A Rock". Or is it "Slip Slidin' Away"? Ah yes, I've got it now. "Still Crazy After All Those Years". That's the one.

∞

### If you thought *that* was hard...

Oh my God, what a day! What an unbelievable, mind-blowingly, gobsmackingly, life-enhancing, death-defying day. A day of Talking Heads songs. "What a Day That Was", "This Must Be The Place", "Psycho Killer". Every last David Byrne lyric seemed to fit this crazy, wonderful day, a day I learned much about myself, more perhaps than I knew existed. Today was way more terrifying, way *way* more terrifying - and thrilling - than even yesterday. A day when, if the mental health authorities had finally gotten around to certifying and sectioning me as completely insane - a process, some might say, that is well overdue - I could surely have had no complaints.

Even when caught up in the very midst of a suicide bombing on the streets of Jerusalem some months ago, the fear, the terror, and most particularly that freeze-dried feeling of staring down the barrel at your own death was not as pronounced as it was today on Mt. Triglav, where eternity seems never to be more than a matter of centimetres away, each skimpy ledge offering the prospect of a fast train to Hades.

This was summit day, and at ten-to-eight on a cold September morning, under brooding clouds that seemed to shake their fist and threaten their worst, Greg and I set off up painfully thin gulleys and along razor-edge ridges for the apex of what I was increasingly aware is one of Europe's most forbidding mountains, more so even than Mt. Blanc, which claims nothing like the lives snuffed out by Triglav.

I swear to God, if I'd known how mean and low-down Triglav was, not only would I have thought twice about taking the job on, but I would certainly have never thought to do so without being fully protected and guided, which I guess moves me down a notch from manically reckless to sadly unwitting. Put simply, neither Greg nor I had the faintest idea what to expect.

As it turns out, and despite the slip-slidey wetness under foot, we reached the summit a full 40 minutes sooner than was projected as the "norm" for getting to the top. We ascribed this to being, perhaps, more accustomed, comfortable even, on this terrain than we would have ever imagined, well prepared by yesterday's induction in moon-walking and iron cable clinging. We even allowed ourselves, fleetingly, to believe that we were brilliant climbers, real macho mountain men who shit behind boulders in all kinds of weather and trample rock and scree like it was so much chopped liver.

We strutted, we preened, we photographed, we high-fived, and we just basked in this moment of victory, before saddling up for the descent down the so-called 'easier' face of the mountain. If we seemed hurried in our moment of glory, it was simply that we wanted to beat the bad weather - the even worse weather - which we sensed was closing in on us. And anyway, it was already cloudy as hell and there was bugger-all prospect of peering across the sky and into Austria and Italy. Plus our hands were getting pretty damn cold. Plus we had no idea how long it would take us to get where we were going. Plus I was busting for a bowel movement, and I make it a rule never to crap above nine-and-a-half-thousand feet. In short, there was little to keep us on Slovenia's rooftop.

Well, what can I tell you? We'd moved barely 10 metres across the summit ridge when Greg calls over with words to the effect of: "Jesus-Holy-Mother-of-Mercy-Christ! What the hell is *that* thing!?"

"Where?" I reply.

"Look up", he says.

"Oh.....fffuck!" I shout, fuck being authentic mountain language and the 'f' lasting just about as long as the sudden, and laughably brief, break in the clouds that reveals...wouldn't you just know it...another peak, a looming, hulking great bastard of a thing, some 600 ft. above us. Not *a* peak, but *the* peak, the object of our toil, sweat, and premature jubilation. And you wonder how we got to the top - the semi-top, the quasi-top, the neo-fake-sorry-just-kidding-and-anyway-can't-you-guys-take-a-joke-top - as quick as we did. We hadn't summited at all. We'd only semi-summited. We were none too pleased. The only reason we weren't thoroughly crestfallen is that we hadn't actually reached the right crest from which to fall. We were, however, and to use Greg's well-chosen choice of poetic licence, pissed as fuck.

We were also humbled. For not only did this fleeting cloud-free moment allow us full view of what was left to scale up ahead, but we managed for the first time to look back down at the full extent of what we'd just come up, which was exactly...*exactly*...the same as lay ahead of us: an almost sheer wall of stark, black rock face, the kind that claims as many victories as it allows, and one, as we were to find out, peppered with memorial stones to fallen climbers.

Did it stop us? Did it heck! We're macho mountain men, me and Greg, and we bounded on up with scarcely another 'fuck', 'shit' or 'damn', and reached the summit - the real summit; no neo, quasi, or fake summit - with over-elaborate care and at a pace that would have a snail rubbing its little hands in joy at finding out he is not, after all, the slowest of all God's creatures. Did I say bounded? OK, crawled.

From the summit - the real, actual summit, Veliki Triglav - we took the North Face descent, the as-it-were 'easier' way down. Easier, bollocks!!! Sly Stallone in *Cliffhanger* would have sweated rivers and lakes on Triglav's North Face. This so-called easier way down filled me with such terror and dread I feel almost cleansed admitting as much. That said, it was also bloody exciting, and the trick with balancing terror and excitement is to make sure the latter outweighs the former,

even if only ever-so-slightly. That way your vibe is that little bit more positive than negative, a jot more 'can do' than 'shit, this is impossible', and with that mindset you're more likely to get through the ordeal, which anyway only ever lasts as long as it takes to reach the relatively calm waters of a slightly flatter, wider bit of terrain.

All of that said, I simply cannot describe this descent into terror in any way that does not sound like gross hyperbole and exaggeration. But the fact is we were, to put it bluntly, on the knife edge to end all knife edges, at times a knife that had no edge. For on some stretches of the ledge - the miserly six-inch wide sliver of path that hugs the mountain with ridiculous intimacy, and flirts with thin air even more capriciously - there was a gap of some three or four feet which we were forced to straddle and stretch just holding on to the iron wall-spikes, the via ferata pitons, whilst trying every which way not to look down at the 6,000 ft. drop over which we all but dangled.

I shiver as I write this, and I shudder in disbelief that the number of fallers, at this point alone, never mind on the entire mountain, doesn't run to hundreds per year. And how easily the census, whatever it stands at, could have been swelled by either Greg or by me. It's a sobering thought, and one I'd sooner have now than then, on Triglav's fearsome 'easier' face.

This suicidal section of mountain endured for the better - perhaps that should be worse - part of two hours, and when, finally, we stepped down on to the loose, carpet-like, gloriously welcoming and criminally overdue Kilimanjaro-type scree, it was with palpable relief as much as reckless abandon that we slalomed down the next four or five hundred feet as though on skis.

Moments later we turned to see what we had left in our wake. Our jaws dropped. We were speechless. It was as much as we could do just to gawp in disbelief at the wonder, the sheer brutality, of the magnificent monster that came quite possibly within an inch of denying us any further involvement in the 21st century. We felt, both of us, humbled, overawed, and unbelievably grateful to still be alive. If there's a God up there in heaven, I do believe he had just done the both of us one huge, whopping great favour.

It would be another six hours - that makes it a 10-hour day - before we hit the valley floor and left the surroundings of the Triglav National Park. This was not as we planned. Blame the crow. Baffled? Read on.

You see, we should, as planned, have traversed the next...oh, I don't know how many...several ridges with a distinct view to fetching up at a refuge at around the 7,000 ft. mark and with a quite unpronounceable name, but undoubtedly involving several Ps, Js, and silent Ks. Instead we took a wrong turn at the foot of the screes. This is where the crow comes in, as I was utterly convinced, and convinced Greg likewise, that in the absence of any alternative intelligence we should head the way directed by the beak on a crow sitting on a rocky outcrop at the convergence of four footpaths. The crow, I felt, was a talisman, something of an omen. Greg called it Damien, the more so as we headed, in the immortal words of Status Quo, down, down, deeper and down.

No matter. The walk, down twisty-turny switchbacks and through densely wooded forest, was gorgeous and peaceful, and we hit the tiny hamlet of Trenta in time for a fish-and-chip supper, a phone call to HumanFish to explain our geographic dyslexia, and a pick-up from one of their guides, Stuart, late of Canterbury, latterly domiciled in Slovenia. Stuart and I, it turns out, have friends in common through our mutual contacts at Exodus, who channel their Slovenia trade through HumanFish, and the three of us while away the remains of the day in a bar back in Bled, supping cappuccinos and red wine, before hitting the pillow back in the Grand Hotel Jadran.

I'm glad I climbed Triglav - of course I am. But should I have? That is the question. With the benefit of hindsight, probably not. I know I've always tended to walk that fine line between fearless and reckless. It might even be one of my defining characteristics; that's for others to say. But this last climb, frankly, had one small toe in fearless, and the other nine in reckless. Never mind the hanging-on-to-the-side-of-a-mountain-by-my-fast-freezing-fingertips bit; just being in the relatively calm waters of the gigantic lunarscape boulders a way below death-ridge, slipping around on their rain-sodden surface, was daft enough.

And if anything had happened to Greg I'd have felt an uncomfortable degree of culpability. The trip itself might have been Greg's initiative - and I'm so glad he invited me to join him. But matters today were very much in my hands. Greg, you see, was clearly in two minds about making the summit attempt in such tricky conditions, weather-wise. I saw it in his face, I heard it in his voice. "What do you reckon, Peter?" he asked over breakfast, as we both gazed out into a dank, dark drizzle that should have been all the answer he needed.

"Ah, what the hell", I said. "Let's do it".

◌ℬ

### Ecstasy is a room above a Croatian bar...

Three things happen when I wake this morning.

One: I realise, on scanning back through the night's activities, that I did not, despite all of Greg's predictions to the contrary, have a falling dream. I was sure I would, so firmly did he plant the idea in my head. And given every falling dream I ever had neither preceded nor presaged a fall of any kind (usually it came just after watching *Vertigo* for the umpteenth time) it seemed Greg might be right. But no. I dream instead of Kate Winslet, a high-back chair and a length of rope.

Two: My thighs, already the worse for wear from far too many knocks and nudges on the football field, are screaming out to me for justice and rest in that what-did-we-ever-do-to-you kind of way that only 3-times-a-week soccer players will understand. Perhaps I didn't explain well enough in yesterdays log the full extent of the stress and strain placed on thighs, knees and calf muscles in stretching from iron spike to iron spike, and over boulders the size of small villages, on the side of a mountain. Even decades of football on the muddy pitches of north-west London are scant preparation for such muscle pummelling.

And Three: I determine to go right out when the shops open and buy myself one of those signs that read: "You don't have to mad to work here, but it helps". I might have to change the words a little, say to: "You don't have to be mad to climb one of Europe's toughest peaks, without harness, ropes or protection of any kind, *and* in wet and slippery conditions, but the fact is you *are* mad, perhaps even certifiably so, as you've undoubtedly been told many times before. SEEK HELP NOW". Of course, I don't buy any such sign - there's no piece of wood large enough - but I hope this illustrates how questionable my sanity seemed by this stage of the proceedings.

"Did anyone ever threaten to shoot you for making a crap suggestion?" I ask Greg as CNN buzzes the morning news into our bedroom.

"Not that I can recall", Greg replies. "Why do you ask?"

"Suggest anything involving walking today", I warn, "and you'll find out".

And so we set off on a walk - a mere 5 miles over largely level ground - around the lake. Bled is a quite beautiful stretch of water that, strangely, loses little in the early morning rain. Certainly the hugely impressive mountain backdrop is totally submerged and utterly lost in a sea of cumulus nimbus. But the little church on Bled Island looks somehow even more magical than usual with its spire piercing the cloud and seeming almost disembodied from the main body of the building.

The changing colours of the leafy overhang was kaleidoscopic, a visual assault of browns and greens, reds and yellows. I'm not so sure I liked the grandstand at the lake's far end, carved as it is into the hillside and spilling down to the lake for purposes of watching rowing events at the Zaka Regatta Centre. But Slovenia is actually rather successful on the water, and if the country's Olympic gold medallists choose to hone their oarsmanship on these waters, then I guess the locals are entitled to watch from a decent vantage point, and never mind my aesthetic bleatings.

Lake Titicaca aside, I have never in my life seen such translucent blue waters as on Lake Bled. This, it seems to me, is due in no small measure to a complete absence of motorised craft of any kind on the waters. The only transport you'll see on the lake are row-boats, kayaks, and the hand-propelled gondolas that ferry the tourists to and from the island. It's all very eco-conscious and very, *very* pretty.

Well, so much for Bled. And no, I don't curse Greg for the walk. My legs, it turns out, have rather more mileage than I was entitled to expect, and all those hours in the gym, on the treadmill, the verti-climber and the leg extension machines, are clearly paying the kind of dividends that could make you a very rich man.....and anyway, we've hired a car.

# CLIMBING SLOVENIA

And so, on the dot of midday we check out of the hotel, into the Opel, and head south to Croatia.

On route we make a small detour to the Skojcan Caves to check out a subterranean, 700 feet-beneath-the-ground underworld of stalagmites, stalactites and thundering rivers and cascades, a simply astounding other-worldly experience straight out of Jules Verne's *Journey to the Centre of the Earth*. We're joined by a party of Israelis, by far the most prolific tourists this particular week in Slovenia, as they seem to be pretty much wherever I go, be it Machu Picchu, the Galapagos Islands, or Stockholm. There are many reasons for this, but now is not the time for such philosophical musings. Suffice to say, for *whatever* reason Israelis are superb travellers and uniquely placed to bring all manner of perspective to their journeying.

From the caves we reach the border within a half-hour or so, and then to the sea-side town of Umag for a late-lunch-early-supper and much animated debate as to exactly what we plan to do in Croatia...and, of immediate importance, where we might hang our hats for the night. We pore over maps, by now lost in a tidal wave of pizza and calzone, and decide to head for the hills, with a view to hiking tomorrow in the apparently very fine mountains of the Risnjak National Park, home, it is said, to some of Croatia's finest and most scenic trekking.

With nowhere to stay - which is to say we've booked nothing in advance - we drive around in the rain, in the dark, in a country of which we know slightly less than nothing at all, until at last we reach a tiny town that gives every impression of having closed down. It's 10 o'clock at night and the town's electricity consumption extends to just one flickering strip of neon over a moody-looking bar, the one and only horse in a one-horse town.

The town is called Delnice and the bar, not unlike Clint Eastwood, is the bar-with-no-name in the town-with-no-people. Actually there was one person in the bar. A girl. A gorgeous, sumptuously proportioned girl who gave me real reason to live. I only saw her top half - she was behind the counter - but it was all I needed to throw myself upon her mercy.

"My friend and I need a room for the night", I said. "Is there a hotel in town?"

She produced a key from the cash till and led me upstairs to the cosiest, cleanest top-of-the-house letting room you could wish for. Comfy twin beds, squashy duvet, colour TV, shower, and a very attractive Croatian girl in a town where no-one else seemed to exist. For a moment I forgot about Greg. You would, wouldn't you?

My memory restored, I call out the window to Greg, who is in the car relying on me to secure some sort of accommodation deal.

"We're in", I say. "$15 a head, breakfast included".

We were very happy, ecstatic even. Such is life on the road. All it takes for high-level ecstasy is some low-grade achievement as finding a bed for the night. When it's cold and wet and pretty damn late and you're tired as fuck, *and* you find the bed is offered you by someone who could pass muster as a Cameron Diaz lookalike and might not be averse to turning your blankets for you...well, I don't have to tell you how easily some folk fall to their knees and find God.

We dumped our stuff, had a quick clean-up, and went down to the bar for a night-cap before retiring to our Croatian attic and a dubbed episode of *The Simpsons*. Sleep came very easily.

**I don't remember asking for boiled vegetables...**

We're breakfasted and out by 8.30 - and no, nothing was turned for us by the Croatian girl, blankets or otherwise - and moments later we're hiking a 6,000 ft. mountain in torrential rain. Through dense forest, over omnibus-sized boulders and fallen trees, all the way to the summit, the climb is fine, but alas no views. We're high above Croatia, but we see nothing beyond the clouds that steal our vista.

The high point of the morning - other than the high point - is tearing around the lower slopes, after the climb, trying to escape the forest along unmarked dirt-tracks in an Opel Corsa that is ill-designed, ill-equipped, and woefully ill-prepared for the Formula One treatment to which I subject the poor thing.

I am - I will say it here and now, loud and clear - a very good driver. No matter that Greg would vigorously argue the point. What he might describe as driving like a man possessed, I call backing out of my drive. My foot pressed to the floor, one hand on the wheel, the other permanently on the radio dial (you have to, if only to escape the ubiquitous Manically Whingeing Preachers, only to find Eminem with the naughty words bleeped out, which is kind of strange since he sings in English and this is Slovenia), I just love driving hard and fast, the more so when it's somebody else's car. I am - truly, truly am - a seriously frustrated and potentially lethal rally driver, and when I'm throwing a car around tight bends on uneven tracks at high speeds I am very happy indeed.

Back on the real road we return to Slovenia past towns and villages with various spellings of the name *Petrin, Petrina* and *Petrinja* to name three, all three of which excite Greg no end. Greg's full name, you see, is Gregory Anton Petrin and, grandparentally speaking, he is one-part Croatian, several parts Slovenian. He is, therefore, and on this particular stretch of the journey, very much at one with this little corner of Europe.

## CLIMBING SLOVENIA

As we drive the rainfall trebles its intensity, and by the time we reach the little village of Ribcev Laz on the shores of Lake Bohinj we are left with near-zero optimism as to what the next few days might hold weather-wise. We check into a cosy Alpine lodge - Slovenia is so much like Switzerland in the chalet sense - and settle ourselves for a meal for which we had waited an awfully long time.

A bowl of distempered mucous arrived at Greg's place setting. It was goulash soup. Possibly goulash means snot in Slovenian. It was tough just looking at it. God alone knows how hungry Greg must have been to actually eat it. What came my way is definitely not what I ordered. I asked for a mushroom omelette with roast potatoes. What I got was a plate of boiled vegetables swimming - no; change that; *drowning* - in what seemed suspiciously like, and quite possibly was, placenta.

It was served by a waitress who seemed oddly determined, for one who had never before met me, to compound my discomfort, and my hunger, by all means possible, primarily her quite astonishingly profound memory loss, especially as regards bread, the ferrying of which to my table was clearly a concept too far at this point in her amnesia. And the mistaking of pecan pie for veal cutlets is a minor miracle of misunderstanding which I hope she will carry with her to her grave. She should see the film *Memento*, the one where Guy Pearce's memory loss is so acute he takes to plastering his body with hand-written notes. If I find out she does that, I'm heading back to the lodge and ordering breast of chicken.

And so to bed, with somebody else's meal still languishing on my table, a rumbling in my belly, and the threat in the sky of yet another day's merry-making in the rain.

‿ℬ

### Capital idea...

Rain...more of it...lots more of it, and not a view in sight to call a photo, even in this most exquisite of Alpine settings. This is what we awoke to. The options are threefold: One: Trek and climb in the driving rain with every prospect of not even once receiving the hard-earned reward of something worth looking at. Two: Kayak, or raft, down river or on the lake in conditions conducive to almost anything other than kayaking or rafting down river or on the lake. Three: Get in the car, drive on out to Ljubljana and check out the Old Town, secure in the knowledge we'll always find succour from the more capricious elements in one or other steamy little café on a backstreet between river and castle. We take the cappuccino route.

And so we drive to Ljubljana, park up in a downtown parking lot, and start walking. Well, for Ljubljana, read Prague Lite. There's no other way to describe it. From the top of the hilltop castle to the mottled reds and yellows, pinks and ochres of the shops and town-houses, via the hordes of backpacking students, Ljubljana is Prague in miniature. This is especially so when you cast a little wider and realise that all this colour and cuteness - and it is undoubtedly very endearing - is confined to a tiny central area, perhaps 600 metres square, while all around the perimeter and into the suburbs is pure pre-Glasnost Moscow, an endless, ugly sprawl of faceless, grey and quite depressingly anonymous apartment blocks, each one identified not by name, but by number...just like Moscow, just like Prague.

The castle is a monumental disappointment. The views are undeniably fine. But the structure is a disaster, original windows long replaced with the kind of clear-glass picture windows favoured by a myriad modern housing estates from Basildon to Stevenage. The centre of town, however, *is* a delight and agreeably top heavy in atmospheric alcoved little cafes, two of which we were happy to grace and attend to our respective jottings.

Slovenia's capital city nailed in half a day, we head back to Bohinj determined that the next two days, regardless of weather, will find us back on our feet and in the mountains. We make for the wooden lodge, the one with the flighty waitress, and settle once more to a supper full of surprises, rich in dishes that may well have been ordered by someone, but most definitely not by us.

Me? I just don't know when I'm beaten. Hence I try once more for a mushroom omelette and roast potatoes. I get fried chicken and chips. My hopes weren't high. The waitress, I think, was. Nutrition value, two-out-of-ten. Entertainment value, off-the-scale. Ah well.

### How many countries can you see...?

At last, blue skies. We jumped out of bed, all but leaping off the balcony, so keen

were we to see Slovenia under gorgeous light and with the sun on our backs.

We'd scarcely finished our breakfast before heading out and up the nearest mountain, improvising ourselves a 9-hour route and hauling ourselves over rock and crag, through dense forest, high above the lake and way above the snow-line, to the 7,000 ft. summit of Mount Prsivec.

It was wonderful, it was beautiful, and it was our reward for infinite patience and resolve in the face of a hitherto horribly rainy onslaught. We climbed in blissful peace and solitude, our only company on route being hundreds of sheep on a grassy outcrop up around the 5,000 ft. mark. The views were to die for, the ones we should have had from Triglav all those days ago. Plus we could see Triglav itself, in all its majesty and in the context of the lesser peaks which it dwarfs so imperiously.

"How many countries can you see?" I called to Greg as we peered down, from opposite ends of the ridge-like summit, across the shimmering blue expanse of Lake Bohinj. It looked so lovely, fringed by lofty pines and framed by mighty peaks.

"That's Slovenia down there", said Greg, "so I guess that's Austria up ahead, and that'll be Italy over to the left, and heaven alone knows where Hungary and Croatia are".

Guesswork perhaps, though educated guesswork. But with a circular 360 degree vista at our disposal, and at a mile-and-a-half in the sky, it's guaranteed, Slovenia being such a tiny wee place, we had at least three countries in view, maybe even four, and who knows, it's just possible all five were out there somewhere between the Adriatic and Budapest.

And so we stood, fully enveloped on all sides by raging beauty, having gained 5,000 ft. in elevation in about as many hours. We felt pretty pleased with ourselves. OK, we hadn't used up any more of our nine lives, nor did this climb necessitate use of our Get Out Of Jail Free Card. Just as well, really. We'd already used it on Triglav. But it was a testing enough haul up the hillside, and four hours later, in a local pizzeria - what; you think we're risking it again with the amnesiac waitress back at the lodge? - we kind of felt we'd earned the enormous portions of correctly delivered supper that flowed our way.

$\infty$

**The priest, the cameraman and the solitary witness...**

I write these words with a chorus of church bells ringing in my head.

While Greg is squeezing one last trek into our last full day in Slovenia, I've just rowed my way across Lake Bled to the tiny island in the middle to sit and gaze across the water towards the splendid castle on top of which I was perched earlier this morning.

The water is bluer than I could have ever imagined blue to be. It has me thinking at once of Miles Davis and Joni Mitchell, of Roy Orbison and The Marcels, and everyone else who ever utilised the word 'blue' in one or other recording. It is achingly beautiful, unutterably bewitching. In fact, it is no longer blue, but a deep, rich, luminescent turquoise; several shades of deep, rich, luminescent turquoise; an *aurora borealis* of deep, rich, luminescent turquoise, the dinky little row boats bobbing up and down and sending ripples of turquoise towards the dinky little jetty, and then away again as they bounce back towards the shore.

The church on Bled Island is an absolute gem, all mottled pinks and lime greens and Roman clock face and big black spire and rising through the trees as though planted rather than constructed, and it seems I have it all to myself...the jetty, the hundred-and-one steps (I know, I counted), the church, the trees, the fluoride-striped parasols that shade the absent hordes. It seems like Paradise, the perfect place to collect my thoughts, the pealing church bells supplanting the ubiquitous chirping of mobile phones by which I usually mull and muse.

And then, up the steps that lead from the jetty to the church, come a bride and groom, complete with entourage. The entourage extends no further than a priest, a cameraman and a solitary witness, who, it turns out, is the cameraman, who will no doubt wield videocam and wedding ring at the same time, for he is the best man too, as I find out when I stand at the back of the church, watching the proceedings with a kind of gooey nostalgia. I cannot imagine a nicer place to get married, an absolute idyll. Where better for two young people to pledge themselves to one another. And where better for one not-so-young person on yesterday's legs to while away the rest of the afternoon, lost in thought under a warm welcoming sun.

I sit a while longer and wonder to myself if I will ever stop travelling, if I will ever tire of life on the road, backpack and passport my constant companions. I consider an existence free of airports, of queuing, of tannoy announcements, unseemly delays, and unscheduled diversions such as took me not so very long ago to Sao Paolo instead of La Paz, and only this week took me and Greg to the foot of the wrong valley on account of my misplaced trust in a crow. I think of my family, who I love, my friends too, and my home. I think of my gym, my football team, my local café, of Brighton and Bournemouth where my daughter and son now live. I think of the Shepherd's Bush Empire, the Brixton Apollo and all the other rock venues I love to visit whenever Elvis Costello or David Byrne or Tom Waits is in town.

And then I think of Andalucia's *pueblos blancos*, the Cosy Corner Beach Bar in Belize, the thrilling mayhem of Marrakech's Djemaa El Fna, and a return to the

# CLIMBING SLOVENIA

Galapagos Islands with, of course, my ubiquitous little short-wave radio (for long-distance soccer results purposes), and I see at once I have my answer. Travel is as much a part of me as the blood that pumps and flows each time I excitedly, and fearfully, cling to the side of a mountain, each time I swim with seal pups and turtles, or peer across the ramparts of an ancient Inca stronghold. It's not something I could ever stop, even if I wanted to, and why would I ever want to? Who could see the Mayan pyramids of Tikal, the salt lakes of Bolivia, or the Berber villages of the High Atlas, and choose to stay in Edgware a moment longer than absolutely necessary? Not me, that's for sure.

And then it's time to row back to the shore and drive down to Bohinj to pick up Greg. He too has had a great day, and I'm glad. We head back to Bled, to the Grand Hotel Jadran, and, showered and changed and sparkly clean, we meet up with Andrazj for a glass of wine and a big fat pasta supper, little aware of the astonishingly blue skies that, at the dawning of tomorrow, will bid us farewell to this lovely, well-kept secret of a country.

And it's those blue skies, of which we'd had such a teasingly small taste, that I have little doubt will tempt me back another time, perhaps to tackle Triglav by a different route, more likely to scour the Slovenian Alps for an even dafter, more hair-brained challenge. Andrazj says there's a peak called Razor - "the perfectly-named mountain" he calls it - that has ledges and ridges to turn your legs to jelly and your brain to liverwurst and makes Triglav, by all accounts, seem like a trip to the dentist.

I like the sound of that. Let's see how my body holds up...and my sanity.

# DIDN'T YOU INSULT MY MOTHER?

There's an old joke that goes something like this:
Customer: "I didn't come here to be insulted!"
Waiter: "So where do you usually go then?"
Maybe it's funny, maybe it's not.  But it's absolutely,
irrefutably, essentially New York.

## Eight great journeys

"I like to watch what I eat", I said to my waiter. "I find I can get more in my mouth that way".

I was in New York City's Carnegie Deli, where a sandwich is not so much a meal as a building site, and pastrami on rye comes with planning permission and a step ladder. I never saw anything like it, sandwiches the size of statues, blintzes the size of bazookas. Stand a Carnegie triple-decker frankfurter special on pumpernickel bread with sweet and sour pickle, coleslaw, sauerkraut and two extra squeezes of Colman's up on its end, alongside Michaelangelo's Statue of David, and take it from me, you would not know the difference.

And heaven help you if you don't finish what's on your plate. The Carnegie trade in guilt. You leave so much as a crumb, the merest seed off your challa roll, or gherkin off your hors d'ouvres plate, and as God is my witness there'll be a waitress swarming all over you like the Jewish mother of your worst nightmares, telling you how to eat, when to eat, where to eat, why to eat, and quite possibly who to eat.

And not just waitresses. Sometimes it'll be another diner comes up to you levelling accusations of under-eating. I've seen it happen. Someone else's mother, some complete stranger from the United States of Mind Your Own Business, will come up to you, the heavenly aroma of kosher dining wafting out of every pore, and assail you with long-forgotten cliches that remind you exactly why it was you left home five minutes after your barmitzvah.

My own eating consultant came in the considerable form of a woman sitting two seats away from me at a shared table. Actually, two, three and four seats away - she was that big, in the way only Americans can be that big. Lose the mascara, add a stetson, and it could have been Hoss Cartwright. I don't mean to be uncharitable - maybe it was something glandular, and being American it was quite possibly hereditary - but the fact is, if this lady were out swimming in the ocean and came nose-to-nose with a great white shark, the shark had better hope he opens his mouth first.

We were destined to meet. I felt that as soon as I saw her across the permanently crowded room, even before I was herded to my seat. She walked round the table in a pair of $500 lizard-skin shoes that I swear she's never seen, so as to get a good position right there behind me. And here she was now, up close and personal, flecks of chopped herring caught in the fleshy crevice between two of her many chins, some of which were flapping in the breeze of her own making, readying herself to offer me the benefit of all her culinary expertise. She leaned forward, her ample bosom having much the same effect on my head as the Crash had on Wall Street, and let me have it:

"YOU'RE NOT EATING PROPERLY, MY LITTLE MUNCHKIN. WHAT'S THE MATTER WITH YOU? YOU DON'T LIKE YOUR FOOD?"

This lady could have woken the dead. I only thank God she didn't have wind; the effects could have been catastrophic.

"I'm fine thanks", I mumbled, with uncommonly good grace. "Really, I'm fine".

## DIDN'T YOU INSULT MY MOTHER?

I wasn't fine. Memories of eating battles with my real mother, the force-feeding of all things green that kick-started a lifetime's rebellion, began to rise to the surface...along with kishkes, knishes, kneidlach, kreplach, and a wedge of potato kugel the size of Nova Scotia.

"FINE?" she hollered, as though I were deaf as well as full. "WHAT FINE? A MAN LEAVES HALF HIS DINNER AND HE TELLS ME HE'S FINE?

I stared down her bosom - it was like staring into the Caves of Altamira - and then down at the table, catching her reflection in my neighbour's chicken soup, quite unable to distinguish her remarkably bulbous nose from a greasy matzo ball that was bobbing to the surface. Now I'm not in favour of face-lifts, so please don't think I'm advocating cosmetic surgery, even for someone this spectacularly grotesque. But when people start to mistake bits of your face for testicular globs of unleavened bread, it's time to go under the knife.

"YOU'RE ANOREXIC, MISTER. THAT'S WHAT YOU ARE; ANOREXIC!"

"Do I look anorexic?" I asked. You notice how it's only the terminally obese who accuse you of serial thinness.

"YES YOU DO!" she bellowed. "YES...", and here she slowed her delivery for maximum theatrical effect..."YES...YOU...DO!"

She put her hands on her hips, thrust out her chest like two juggernauts in a logjam of Ford Fiestas, and proceeded to do the thing I dreaded most. She softened her voice, the calm before the storm, in that I'm-Margaret-Thatcher-and-you-know-you-can-trust-me kind of a way.

"Yes you do", she repeated, all sweetness and light. "You look *very* anorexic".

"I don't think so", I said. For surely, in the circumstances - the circumstances being that I'm five-foot-nine, one hundred and sixty pounds, and really rather well-muscled - this is all that needed to be said.

"HEY, MISTER!" she screeched. Her face, by now, was so close to mine she could reach inside my ear with her tongue, have a wander up and down my nasal cavity, and perhaps even check out some recent root canal work. "MISTER!" she repeated. "SOMEBODY OUGHTA TEACH YOU HOW TO EAT PROPERLY!"

This was rich, coming from someone whose face looked like the unswept floor of a kosher butcher after a particularly busy day hacking and chopping wildfowl and sheep.

"Madam", I replied, with all the hauteur I could muster. "I, at least, manage to get my food *inside* my face".

She was about to start in again, but I had the presence of mind - I'm not proud to admit this, because even under the most severe duress I try and remain every inch the perfect gentleman - but yes, I do admit, I showed her the finger, two fingers, one from each hand, thrust upwards with extreme prejudice.

"And madam", I said, affecting the upper class tones that Michael York stole from James Mason all those years ago. "If your husband should decide to go down on you in the middle of the night, do please make sure he finishes what he's eating, every last bit, *with* the appropriate blessing before and after.

She retreated to the pay desk, tail firmly between her voluminous legs, I asked for the bill, and that seemed to be that...or so I thought. For something then happened that, if I live to be a hundred and ten, I seriously believe will haunt me every time I go in, or near, an Upper East Side delicatessen. Mrs Irma Finklestone - for by now I had decided that this was her name - charged back to my table like a buffalo on heat, raised her arm as though to strike me dead, and proceeded, with a lightness of touch that was hugely impressive for one so enormous, to swipe what remained of my potato kugel off my plate and into her pocket.

I was impressed.

I settled my account and emerged from the restaurant much clearer as to why Woody Allen filmed *Broadway Danny Rose* in the Carnegie. More eating, less talking. You get the actors cheaper that way. In fact, I was altogether clearer as to why Woody is so reluctant to make movies beyond the confines of his beloved Manhattan. The place positively throbs with life. There is nothing you cannot do, see, buy, visit, encounter, embrace, fondle or eat at any time of the day or night, in New York. And it's big...my, but it's big... and about as understated as a Halle Berry acceptance speech. That episode in the Carnegie - which was as far from understated as you'll ever get; it just wouldn't happen in any other town. It's pure New York.

Megalopolis. That's what Allen Ginsberg called Manhattan, and that's just what it is. A truly mega metropolis where everything is larger than life. But more than that - and here's the rub - it's so Jewish, the most Jewish town on the planet. Statistics don't lie, and with well over two million Jews in residence that's upwards of 15 per cent of world Jewry living in the one city. And you wonder why New York is so noisy.

The Carnegie Deli? New York has a hundred and one Carnegie Delis, from Katz's to Lindy's, from Kaplan's at The Delmonico to Sammy's Famous Rumanian Restaurant, and all of them quintessentially Jewish places where you can get insulted and abused absolutely free of charge, *and* raise your cholesterol levels to hitherto uncharted heights. Take it from me, a Jew driving in New York City will never be stopped by the police for drinking, only for overeating. And when he's been

stopped, do not expect a courteous rebuke and an apologetic response. Instead, sit back and just watch the insults fly. Walking down Seventh Avenue I heard the following rapid-fire exchange between a traffic cop and a native obviously Jewish New Yorker:

Cop: "Your tax is outa date".

Jew: "Get outta here! You're still wearing flares".

A classic New York exchange. Short, sharp, straight-to-the-point, and delivered with the timing of a Jack Benny or a Billy Crystal. What Americans lack in irony they more than make up for by way of sarcasm, and don't let anyone tell you otherwise. American abuse, and in particular American-Jewish abuse, is so much better than anything we Brits can offer, so much healthier, out there, in-your-face. The verbal haranguing I received in the Carnegie? That was great stuff, not your Basil Fawlty-type invective, borne of a deeply repressed psyche, a miserable-but-never-discussed adolescence, and a lifetime's unresolved angst, otherwise known as being British. What I got in the deli was plain, old-fashioned, honest-to-goodness rudeness, the birthright of the Jewish people as handed down to Moses on Mount Sinai...along with the Ten Commandments, the blueberry cheesecake, and a hardback manual called *Overbearing and Overeating : A Beginner's Guide to Being Jewish*. This is healthy stuff.

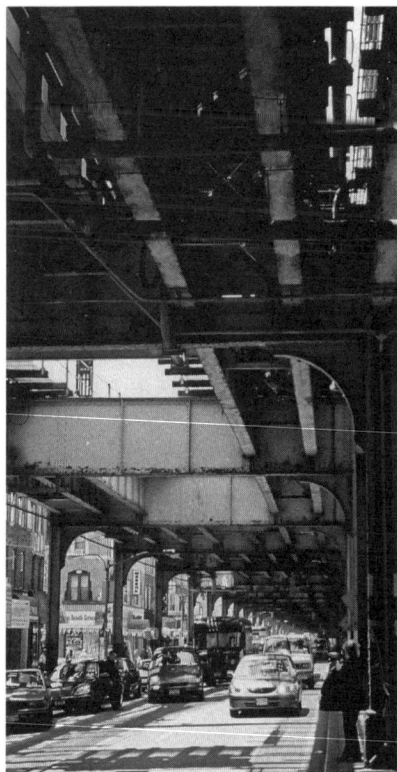

What can I tell you? Since the dawning of time, or 1492 at least, travellers have come to Manhattan from all around the world just to be insulted in a Jewish delicatessen. I've seen people come out of the Carnegie and actually complain when the staff treated them nicely. This is not the Carnegie way. And what's more, what I got at the Carnegie was like an audience with the Pope compared with what's on offer at the Second Avenue Deli. Down on Second Avenue the rudeness of the men and women in starched white linen is the stuff of legends, as I discovered on a recent visit.

My whitefish - that's America-speak for what the rest of us know as gefilte fish - looked awful. I don't know how long it had been lying dead before it was scooped up and put on my plate, but I'd say its family had long gotten up from sitting shiva and already were planning the stone-setting. If it were a person, and not a slab of congealed carp, you'd be lecturing it in the joys of personal hygiene. This was not a piece of fish you wanted to hobnob with and take home to meet your parents. It was, amongst the fish community, a social pariah. Even the little sliver of carrot perched on top was trying every which way to slide down towards the calmer waters of the horseradish sauce. It was, in a word, putrid. I called the waitress over.

This was the waitress from hell. You remember the film *Deliverance*, that scene where Ned Beatty takes it from behind up against a tree from some inbred backwoodsman with a plaid shirt and no front teeth? She looked like the tree. Of all the waitresses in all the delis in all the world, I get served by The Golem of the Lower East Side.

She swaggered over, remarkably John Wayne-like for a skinny old bird, her mouth a minor miracle of synchronicity as it masticated a stick of Wrigleys and a dog-end of Marlborough Light in perfect harmony. I braced myself for a fight, then let her know as un-Britishly as I could that I was not happy.

"I don't like the look of my whitefish", I said.

"If it's looks you wanted", she replied, a great swab of ash dropping into my borscht, "you shoulda ordered gold!"

"Didn't you insult my mother?" I replied. But she was gone, doubtless to spit invective on another hapless punter like some Benzedrine-fuelled viper.

It was time for a bit of culture. Now let me say at once, museums and galleries are not my thing. From Rodin's *Thinker* to the drippings of Jackson Pollock via the gigantic Inca phalluses of Lima's Gold Museum, historical artefacts just don't ring my bells, particularly when housed in overheated, under-ventilated exhibition halls. Frankly I'd sooner see a movie. But give me somewhere with Jewish interest, a place where I might make sense of my own blighted history - which excites, intrigues and infuriates me in roughly equal measure - and I'm happy as a parochial Jew in a parochially Jewish museum.

One such museum - and it's worth a visit just for that classic New York view across the river to Ellis Island and The Statue of Liberty - is the Museum of Jewish Heritage down on Battery Park.

They say Steven Spielberg helped bank roll the museum; part of his own personal post-Schindler's List Jewish journey, apparently. Well, more power to him, and to everyone else associated with this wonderful enterprise.

It truly is an outstanding museum, a majestically conceived and affectingly recounted story of Jewish life through the ages, with real emphasis on the twentieth century. Not enough museums focus on the recent past, as though recent is somehow *too* recent to be regarded as history. And heaven knows this applies in trumps to formal religious Jewish education which, in my experience, dwells too long and too deep on the dim, distant and fanciful past of the Old Testament, lest

# DIDN'T YOU INSULT MY MOTHER?

we supplant mythical tales of destroyed temples and Red Sea crossings with the hard facts of the Holocaust and the establishment of the State of Israel.

The Museum of Jewish Heritage, on the other hand, pitches it just about perfect, offering a comprehensive journey through modern Jewish history on a highly accessible scale, and the Holocaust retrospective in particular is a model of economy and understatement and, in its own way, more moving even than Yad Vashem in Jerusalem and an object lesson in visual presentation.

Now I'm not an emotional person, or if I am I don't always show it. But I felt wretched to my very core as I watched one particular item of archived newsreel, the images as compelling as they were graphic. A brother and sister, no older than my own children, stand helplessly and hopelessly by as their parents are led towards extermination in Bergen-Belsen. The boy's body is slumped forward, his head in is hands, one eye peering through a crack he has made in his fingers, trying both to coo and not to see his parents being taken away from him. The girl tries to scream out, but no sound is heard. She is literally dumbstruck. I tried everything in my power, but I simply could not shift from my mind the nightmare notion that these were my own children, as they might so easily have been were I but a single generation older than I am. What a terrible image to conjure in your own mind. And what a perfectly good reason for us to be reminded, through exhibits and education and museums such as this, about a period of frighteningly recent history from which we seem, thus far, to have learned so little.

The Museum of Jewish Heritage is a stunning contrast of darkness and light. As you step away from scenes of desolation in the death camps towards the window, you are suddenly regaled with that magnificent view to the Statue of Liberty. In a matter of inches you're taken from doom-laden oppression to the Land of the Free, quite unable to figure whether you're on the inside looking out or, more appropriately for a people whose psyche is so deeply rooted in paranoia, the outside looking in.

Step a few feet the other way from the Holocaust exhibit and you have an even greater contrast, the video-screened Who's Who Who's Jewish in the World of Entertainment. What an absolute riot. I thought it was just British Jews who played "Claim The Jew". If you don't know Claim The Jew, this is when someone - say The Pope, Elvis Presley, Ronnie and Reggie Kray - who never once in their life said they were Jewish, and almost certainly isn't Jewish, hits the front pages for whatever reason, even reasons of notoriety. And the moment he hits the front pages we Jews decide that he must be Jewish.....in The Pope's case because he's Polish, in Elvis' case because his middle name is Aaron, and in the Krays' case because they were once seen in the East End of London eating bagels.

This phenomenon derives partly from the fact that these guys are famous, and we Jews are just about insecure enough, not to say presumptuous, to believe that anyone famous, famous even for all the wrong reasons, simply must have some Jewish blood in him. Even when they were born Jewish, before diluting their blood with Baptism - say Benjamin Disraeli, or Bishop Montefiore - we continue to clutch them to the Seder service of our bosom, dismissing their rejection of, and removal from, Judaism with a smile, a shrug, and a "that's-no-job-for a-nice-Jewish-boy". But mostly it's because our numbers are dwindling - just 13 million worldwide - and we'll take anyone we can. Then the Jewish Chronicle can do a feature on him, unearth an Uncle Harry, perhaps a random synagogue visit for the barmitzvah of the son of a business associate...and that's it, we've Claimed the Jew.

Mostly we claim famous tennis players of the Chilean and Argentinian variety, and sometimes British politicians who are known not to have spoken out against Israel (which narrows it down a bit). We've even claimed the odd extended member of our own Royal family, ascribing to Princess Anne a second husband of Anglo-Judeo background. Charlie Chaplin was Jew For a Day, so too Cary Grant, and even Madonna periodically graces our hit list, based, I can only assume, on her sporadic appearances at celebrity Kabbalah sessions, which I guess makes Mick Jagger Jewish too.

Mickey Most, the one-time pop impresario, was once claimed as Jewish for duality of reason - he lived in Totteridge, a wealthy north London suburb, and Most, surely, was nothing more or less than a thinly veiled Anglicization of Moscowicz via Moss. Most bizarre of all - more so even than claiming Alice Cooper, Lemmy from Motorhead, and the three original members of ZZ Top (who at least have long beards) - more bizarre than any of those, the Jewish press once claimed...you're not going to believe this, but it's true...David Koresh, the cult killer from Waco Texas, on account of someone worked out that 'Koresh' is some kind of brilliantly conceived anagram of Kosher. Well I ask you.

But hold on there. Look who the Museum of Jewish Heritage have claimed, framed and deified. Woody Guthrie was Jewish? The man from Okemah, Oklahoma, the folk movement's working class hero of the Depression years, author of "Pastures of Plenty" and "Dust Bowl Refugees", had a bris, a barmitzvah, and a fistful of blintzes? I find that hard to believe. Sure, we've had the odd protest singer, but usually we're protesting against the price of carpet, not the wage structure of arable farmers in South Dakota. And Harrison Ford? Come on guys, who are you kidding. No self-respecting Jew calls himself Indiana, not even for 10 million dollars a movie. They might just as well claim Michael Jordan. Well why not? There's a river in Israel called...ah, what the hell, you get my point.

I gave over the better part of the morning to the Museum of Jewish Heritage, before stretching my legs and heading down to the Lower East Side Tenement Museum between Broome and Delancey. This gem of a find is actually little more than a 6-storey tenement house, preserved in original layout and condition, which at one time was occupied by 150 mittel-European immigrants. Six apartments, 150 inhabitants. Work it out for yourself. What must it have been like to be a Jew in New York at the turn of the last century, arriving in a land paved with gold, skyscrapers and ghettos on an unfeasibly large and unmanageable scale, half a million Jewish immigrants shoe-horned into an insular inner-city slum?

And what a location. Anywhere less prepossessing you could not imagine. I came out the museum, wandered up and down the street, peering into bars and dives that were almost certainly dens of the most iniquitous kind, with who knows what going on behind shuttered windows and guarded entrances. It remains to this very day one of life's enduring mysteries that in the fifteen or so minutes I strolled back and forth on Orchard Street, not once did I see anyone called Louie or Lefty spill out on to the sidewalk, tearing at each others throats over a floozie called Lulubelle.

I love the Lower East Side. It might be borderline trendy these days and gentrifying at a rate of knots, but it still has an ethnic mix like nowhere else I know. If you've never been to Hanoi, Puerto Rico or Naples, don't bother; it's all there for you between East Houston and the Bowery.

Strange, really. At home I don't see the inside of a synagogue from one Yom Kippur to the next. Give me another book to write and I'll tell you why. And yet, wherever I travel, from Bali to Bolivia via all points marked with a cross, I sniff around for any trace of Jewishness I can find. A mezuzah perhaps, the local synagogue - if one ever existed - or maybe the memorial plaque to a synagogue long-ago destroyed, or simply rendered redundant through lack of a latter day Jewish community.

I've managed to find an Israeli-owned internet cafe halfway up a mountain in the Peruvian village of Agua Caliantes, and an Israeli-owned felafel bar in downtown La Paz. I've exchanged words of Hebrew with a Kilimanjaro mountain guide whose brother-in-law was a kibbutz volunteer right down the road from my kids' old school in the Carmel Mountains. I've even found a Jewish tombstone barely a thousand feet from the 21,000 foot summit of Chimborazo way up in the Ecuadorian Andes, to say nothing of a Hebrew menu in the Moon Rise Café in Puerto Ayora on the tiny and remote Galapagos island of Santa Cruz .

You can imagine, then, that in a town as Jewish as New York I fairly overdose on Yiddishkeit, and before long I was on a ferry to Ellis Island to visit the Museum of Immigration which, at eight years and $156 million, made this restoration the longest in time and the most expensive of any building in the USA. It was worth every last cent. Walking down the "Staircase of Separation", which traces the steps of immigrants who were directed to Manhattan bound ferries, California bound trains, or detention rooms on the island, I had this overwhelming sense of deja vu for a period in history that clearly has no less affected me for my not being there at the time.

OK, I'm not a ritually observant Jew. And yes, my belief in God is entirely conditional upon his showing himself in Bedfordshire in shorts and boots and scoring the goal that gets my beloved Luton Town Football Club up and out of Second Division of the Football League. But there was never a passage of our history, even the ones that occured so long ago I can scarcely view them as credible, that has failed to touch me in some way or another. And that's exactly what New York does to me. It gets right inside me, goes straight to the heart of my Jewish soul, as much my spiritual homeland as Israel, and with a lot less aggrevation.

I guess that's why I decided to spend my Saturday morning in synagogue. I made straight for the Temple Emanu-El on Fifth Avenue, a mightily impressive Romanesque-Byzantine style edifice which, appropriately for so liberal an institution, could not possibly look or feel any less Jewish than it does. Should you wish to visit this synagogue and you're not Jewish, don't worry. This is the one synagogue, New York's largest, where being Jewish is virtually no advantage at all. With my own orthodox background - I've rejected most of it, but at least I know what I've rejected and it's there if I need it - I felt positively rabbinical in a building that is one part mausoleum, nine parts cathedral, and named, for God's sake, after a 1970s soft pornographic movie.

Firstly, I was the only male present to wear any kind of head-covering, and that includes the rabbi. And secondly, I was almost certainly the only person amongst the entire congregation who could read Hebrew. I don't know this for a fact, but since the service contained not one single, solitary word of our ancient language of prayer, what else was I to conclude? Even the Torah scrolls remained firmly in the Ark throughout the service - evidence, if it were needed, that neither the rabbi nor the cantor were any more conversant with Hebrew than their congregants. A synagogue service without Hebrew, frankly, is tantamount to Catholicism without confession, Christianity without the collection.

Synagogues come no more liberal than Temple Emanu-El. Give the caretaker $10 and he'll valet park your car for you. $20 and the rabbi does it. At the post-service kiddush I took the rabbi to task. I asked him how it was that today of all days, when the Torah reading was one of the most important in the whole calendar, the reading of the Ten Commandments, he kept the scrolls firmly under lock and key. The answer he gave is one I shall never forget.

"To tell you the truth", he said, "The Ten Commandments aren't all they're cracked up to be".

I was taken aback.

"The fact is", he continued, "we Liberal Jews believe in the Ten Commandments, but we believe you can pick five".

His sides shook with laughter, he tipped me a wink, and I headed off out to Brooklyn to see my friend Sean get married.

&#x2767;

I met Sean in Peru, the autumn of 1988. He and his pal Don were trekking the fabled Inca Trail to Macchu Picchu, I was trekking the Inca Trail too, so we decided to hitch up, pool our resources, and trek together. Since then, and despite the ocean that separates our respective homes, Sean has become, and remained, as close and valued a friend as I could wish for. And this afternoon he was to be married, in Brooklyn, at the beguilingly gorgeous St. Augustine's Roman Catholic

# DIDN'T YOU INSULT MY MOTHER?

Church on Sixth Avenue, an edifice, and indeed religious experience, for which the Temple Emanu-el provided such solid preparation.

Let me say at once, I think Manhattan is the most remarkable place I know. I'm not saying it's good, I'm not saying it's bad, and frankly it's both. But whatever else it is, it *is* remarkable, a place of raw nervous energy, the kind of place that appeals to those tortured and restless souls who exist on a diet of raw nervous energy. But...and this really is quite a big but...next time you're in New York City, stay in Brooklyn. As a devout worshipper of noise, pollution, carbon monoxide, skyscrapers, madness, mayhem and all manner of record-breaking decibel levels - in other words Manhattan - I realise this statement is little short of heretical. But take it seriously, I urge you.

It may be just a ten minute subway ride from Broadway, Macy's and the Empire State Building, but Brooklyn exists in a world of its own, a world of 19 century brownstone villas, tree-lined avenues, massively and ethnically diverse neighbourhoods, and, in Prospect Park, the most wonderful inner city expanse of forests and meadows, streams and waterfalls I've ever seen, like Hampstead Heath with flat bits.

I spent my lunchtime wandering the literary streets of the Prospect Park neighbourhood with literary guide book in hand. I peered into the basement walk-down on Willow Street where Truman Capote wrote "Breakfast at Tiffany's", right across from where Arthur Miller penned "Death of a Salesman" and offered matzo

ball soup to Marilyn Monroe, allegedly. And many are the works of Henry Miller that are said to have been dredged up in Tom's Diner down on Washington Avenue.

Ah, Tom's Diner, immortalised in song by Suzanne Vega and purveyors of challa French toast drenched in more than enough maple syrup and cinnamon butter to raise your cholesterol levels to heart-breaking heights. I love Tom's Diner. It is, perhaps, my favourite eaterie in all of New York, an old-fashioned, down-home diner with a true rock-and-roll vibe, plus they bring you home-made cookies and fresh orange slices to while away the hour it often takes to queue around the block before finding a seat in the inner sanctum under the beatific smile of Gus, the avuncular proprietor.

Well, the wedding was wonderful. Sean and Catherine looked every inch the beautiful couple they are, Sean's own classical compositions were played by a string quartet as bride and groom walked down the aisle to be blessed by the priest, and the reception in the park found me intemperately, but happily, the worse for Chardonnay, the more so as the party moved on at midnight to Mooney's Irish bar down on Flatbush and Atlantic Avenue and right around from my little brownstone B & B - Brooklyn is rich in cosy brownstone B & Bs - on Sterling Place.

This, I'd have to say, is what I love most about Brooklyn. The place names. Everywhere you go evokes a small-but-significant slice of contemporary music-and-movie history. Say Atlantic Avenue and I think of The Average White Band singing that self same song at the old Rainbow Theatre in rocking Finsbury Park. Show me Grand Prospect Hall and I see Jack Nicholson leering and sneering his way through *Prizzi's Honour*. Walk beneath the elevated railway at Bensonhurst and I defy your mind to picture anything other than Gene Hackman chasing the baddie in *The French Connection*. And Brighton Beach is Neil Simon, pure and simple.

I whiled away many happy hours riding the overland subway across the borough. The photographic possibilities just a few feet above ground level in Brooklyn are endless, stations like Neck Road looking as though they were designed centuries before trains were even invented. The Q-Line from Flatbush to Coney Island is a particular joy, and my walk from Coney Island to Brighton Beach was like strolling along the banks of the Black Sea. So pronounced is the Soviet presence in the area they call Little Odessa - it really is impossibly rich in one-time refuseniks who struggled so long for their exit visas from the old Soviet Union - that English is now all but a foreign language down along the boardwalk, where virtually every last bar and café is called Svetlana, Tatiana or Ludmilla.

To stroll along the boardwalk is to define the word 'evocative'. So many memories, scenes and images - some real, some imaginary - washed over me as I meandered under a baking early summer sun. Memories of my own journeys to and from the Soviet Union back in the early 80s, bringing moral support and everyday basic necessities to Jewish Muscovites and Leningradites, whose desire to express their Jewish identity had rendered their lives intolerable at the hands of the fearsomely, and misguidedly, anti-Semitic regime.

And now, two decades later, they're here, on the boardwalk, playing chess and drinking lemon tea through a cube of sugar clenched between their dazzling new dentures. I reached into my backpack for my camera. And as I did so a bevy of

## DIDN'T YOU INSULT MY MOTHER?

leather-skinned old yentas posed for me. I could tell that once upon a time, perhaps not so very long ago, some of these ladies were really rather beautiful. Now they looked weathered, if not actually withered, by the sun and by the interminable

strain put upon them by their former motherland, the kind of parenthood that makes you happy to become an orphan. They asked me my name. "Peter", I said. "I knew a Peter once", one of them said in thickly-accented English. "Many years ago, before all of...." and she just trailed off, lost in thought, the "before all of..." left hanging in the air, a sentence that had no need to be finished, as I very well understood.

And so, Sunday morning. Brunch with Sean, Catherine, Don, the whole crew from the wedding party, at a hi-tech diner - and I'm not at all sure the words 'hi-tech' and 'diner' really work together - down by the Fulton Ferry State Park, a tiny wee patch of grass, truly no larger than my own back garden, that nestles snugly between the Brooklyn and Manhattan Bridges and stares full-on at the achingly sad void where once stood two glistening, iconic towers across the water.

We ate ourselves silly, before ambling over to the water's edge to drink in the view and, not for the first time in New York, I knew how it felt to be on the set of a Woody Allen movie. Then Greg and I - that's Greg who I would climb with in Slovenia some months later - walked across the bridge and into Manhattan for a little dessert, some genuine street food, the al fresco delights that render Manhattan not so much a borough as a gigantic, constantly evolving delicatessen.

And that, when all is said and done, is what New York is - one big crazy delicatessen where everyone, regardless of race or religion, talks Jewish, liberal rabbis excepted. You know the old story. A Jewish guy is served in Kaplan's by a Yiddish-speaking Chinese waiter. The guy pays the bill and congratulates the manager on the waiter's faultless Yiddish. "Not so loud", says the manager. "He thinks he's learning English".

It would be easy to surmise from all this that New York, Jewish New York in particular, is all about eating. There's a reason for this. It is, pretty much. At the last count New York had 48 eateries with the word *heimesche* in the name, 72 with the word *kosher*, and 129 with the word *bagel*. Even the ice cream of Ben & Jerry adheres strictly to Jewish dietary laws, an object lesson if ever there was one in koshering your assets.

But if the heartbeat of New York lies anywhere, it lies on the streets. I was standing with Greg on the corner of 48th and Park, having made my selection from four of the city's ubiquitous street-corner food stalls, one on each corner. I fancied something hot and sweet so I ordered some lockshen pudding with raisins. Among the raisins I found an insect. "Hey", I said, "there's a fly in my pudding".

The proprietor came back quick as a flash. "What do you expect?", he said. "I used to be a tailor".

Welcome to the Big Bagel.

# MOROCCAN ROLL

Mountains are forbidding places at the best of times, and climbing them can be a humbling experience. I'm not altogether sure whether sharing your sleeping arrangements with an incessantly farting Australian called Bazza makes matters better or worse.

## Eight great journeys

September 2001. It was a week before my birthday, and for as long as I can remember I have spent my pre-birthday week in Morocco. No particular reason. It's a habit that's just sort of stuck, and it's a habit I'm more than happy to stick with a while longer. Marrakech, it so happens, is probably my favourite town...anywhere. And The High Atlas is certainly my favourite mountain range...anywhere. Not the highest mountains I've scaled - not by a long chalk - but certainly the most alluring, seductive and downright beautiful, the pinks and ochres a continuation of that self-same colour scheme that so defines Marrakech. So if that's why I choose Morocco to help me deal annually with the ageing process, go tell me I'm wrong.

This, though, was no ordinary September. The 2001 tells you that much. Never mind that the imminent birthday in question was the one seeing in my half-century on this planet. This was *that* September, the 9/11 September, when we had all of us been overtaken by events too tragic for words. The world was deemed, now more than ever, a dangerous place to be, and air travel in particular was regarded by some to be at best capricious, at worst foolhardy, not least for a Jew coming down to Earth in a Moslem country with a score and more Israel stamps in his passport.

Reason enough to go, don't you think.

&#8449;

And so we arrived as night began to fall, ten of us, complete strangers, drawn together from all ends of the six main continents and thrown together for an attempt to climb to the rooftop of North Africa. We were at the ski resort of Oukaimeden, two miles in the sky and already, even in the last throes of summer, with a dusting of snow. It looked so pretty, more Alpine than Moroccan, ski chairs and T-bars dangling limply from overhead cables that had been pretty much idle since the last winter season.

Sleeping four to a dorm in the musty old ski lodge, I swapped the relentless bottom burps of my bunk-mate Bazza - why do Australians fart so much? - for the somewhat more soothing sounds of Jean Luc Ponty. As Bazza blew himself to the land of nod with a rattle and hum, my headset eased me to bye-bye land at the touch of a button and the heavenly strains of "Cosmic Messenger". London-Casablanca-Marrakech-Oukaimeden in a day, I was ready to sleep. And sleep I did.

&#8449;

Waking next morning to the sound of The Clash singing "London Calling" - actually it was Bazza still farting; funny how you can mistake farting for The Clash - I forwent the undoubted charms of a vat of porridge that, frankly, looked a little too much like the kind of polystyrene goo that holds your ceiling tiles in place, and psyched myself instead for our first acclimatisation climb over the crags and boulders that comprise Jebel Oukaimeden. But first I needed to ask Bazza a question.

"Bazza, why?"

"Why what?" he replied.

"Why do you fart so much?"

"Do I?" he asked.

"You know you do, and if you don't…well…I wouldn't wait around too long for those party invitations to roll in.

"Sorry mate, I never knew", he said, and then proceeded to bang out a belter that could level Oaklahoma.

"Which part of Oz are you from then? Pooh Corner?"

"Pooh Corner?" he asked, deadpan and worryingly vague. "Where's that, mate?" It occurred to me at this point that Bazza might be seriously brain damaged.

"Obviously", I said, summoning all the literary hauteur I could muster, "you never read Winnie-The-Pooh".

"Winnie-The-Pooh?" he said. "Isn't that what Nelson Mandella calls his old lady?"

I saw at once I couldn't compete. I was out of my depth, my eyes were fairly streaming from the effects of Bazza's hyper-active anal glands, plus he came up with a gag I'd have killed for. Bazza slapped me on the back, uttered something to the effect of "you're a good sport mate, and don't let any bastard tell you otherwise", and together we joined the others.

We trooped out the ski lodge and proceeded to shin down the mountain to around the 8,000 foot mark, before scrambling back up to 11,000 ft - that's seriously high for your first day in the mountains - and finally back down again, this time into a gorgeously sheltered valley of sun-bathed beauty and rare tranquillity. And if we were knackered after a gruelling 6-hour morning…well…our fatigue was as nothing compared with our surroundings - a circular wall of 14,000 foot peaks that enveloped us like some kind of gigantic granite charm bracelet.

Over a picnic lunch of couscous, salads, walnuts and couscous,

Mohammed, our head guide, briefed us for what was to come. "This is the easy day", he announced. "Tomorrow it gets harder, and the day after harder still, and the day after…" This is not what we wanted to hear, not after six hours of hauling ourselves and our backpacks over enough jagged and rugged land formations to build an entire new sub-continent.

Mohammed, on the other hand, sashayed around the mountains like Robert Duvall in *Apocalypse Now*. We were his boys, he loved the smell of couscous in the morning, and together we were going to give the enemy a good old British style hiding, trousers down, six of the best, crampons showing if necessary. The enemy was Mount Toubkal, at 14,200 ft the highest peak in North Africa and with some sections so steep you get a nosebleed just reading the cross-section map.

Lunch done, we trekked another four hours, up and down dales, across and over ridges, before fetching up at the climbers' refuge in the precariously balanced village of Tachdirt (pronounced *Tacky Dirt*, and rightly so). If the village clung to the mountainside for dear life, then we clung to dim and distant memories of sanitation for all we were worth. The rat droppings were not a good sign. Neither, it must be said, were the rats. The only reason they were in the refuge in the first place - and let me say here and now, I commend them for their discernment and pragmatism - is that the outdoor toilet was too unsanitary even for the scummiest of God's furry rodents.

The hole in the floor - for that is what the toilet was - was so damn full it was not so much a hole as a hillock. It looked like Mount Etna. Steam was coming off it, for God's sake. What ever happened to civilization? God knows I'm no snob in these matters. I've pissed over mountain ledges, crapped behind rocks, I once even broke wind - and loudly - at a wedding. It was *my* wedding, so you'll understand I was nervous; not so nervous, though, that I didn't blame the rabbi. But the fact is, this toilet in Tacky Dirt was more basic than Jeffrey Archer's grasp of the truth.

All I needed now was for some local kid to try and sell me a luridly ornate dagger encrusted with what looked suspiciously like fossilised shit. I was tired, I was busting for a bowel movement I just knew I'd have to contain until close-to-bursting point, and I most definitely was not up for buying a dagger-in-fossilised-shit, or fossilised anything. How do these people find me?

"OK", I said, weary as hell. "How much?"

His reply, I urge you to believe, came with not a trace of irony. "$150. But for you I make special price".

"How special?" I asked.

"$145", he replied, heroically stoical for one so rooted in a world of fantasy. My God; this kid wasn't even five. I was being fleeced by sperm!

"Come back when you've learned how to haggle", I said, mustering all the authority needed in fending off such a hard-boiled foetus. "You're entering a world of pain", I thought to say, John Goodman's immortal line in *The Big Lebowski* flitting in and out of my head every time someone pisses me off. But I didn't say it. Instead I affected mock anger and righteous indignation, both tinged with a degree of irony as I am neither righteous nor very good at expressing anger.

"Offer him $5", I was advised by Brahim, our other guide. "That's the only way to lose him".

I closed the deal at $2, before selling the thing on to a member of another climbing group for $10.

&#8466;

Brahim - who for some obscure reason I'd taken to calling Brian - woke us four the next morning for what was to prove to be quite the most sensational day's trekking in the High Atlas.

Refreshed from a surprisingly good night's sleep - an unlikely prospect, to judge from my mattress, which was as sickly grey, lumpy and infested as the porridge back at Oukaimeden - we beat a sensuously twisty-turny path around the valleys, up and over vertigo-inducing passes, and all of this under a sky of astral loveliness and the purest pure blue you ever saw. We traipsed through natural coloured Berber villages that dissolve into the scenery so seamlessly you have to look twice to see they're there. They look for all the world as though they grow organically from the hillside, and I don't believe I have anywhere seen such a perfect blend of natural and man-made landscape, the layered Berber houses merging with the stepped crop terraces in perfect union.

Six of our party, it transpired, were teachers. This often seems to be the way on treks, and if anyone knows why this should be, I would very much like to know. Experience - and, to a certain extent, marriage - has taught me to be wary of teachers on holiday, or anywhere. They - and I mean no disrespect to my wife, Susan, who spent many years in the teaching trade - find it mighty hard to let go of the day job.

To this very day I fear if I were unable to satisy Susan sexually, she might make me stand in a corner of the bedroom writing out one hundred times the line: "I *will* enable my wife to achieve multiple orgasm on demand". And on the High Atlas trek I had this constant nagging feeling that if I lagged behind the group to any noticeable extent, I would be made to stand behind a rock with my hands on my head.

One of our teachers was the image of Russell Crowe in *Gladiators*, right down to the loin cloth and immense quadiceps. Her name was Helen. As we walked together, miles ahead of the group - teachers are a powerful laxative for the legs, and exercise in me a strong desire to avoid standing outside staff rooms inhaling stale marijhuana - she exhorted me to (and I quote) "pay attention to the surroundings and concentrate a little less on the other lasses on the trek", and I knew at once that the spirit of Joyce Grenfell was alive and well and living in Cleethorpes, or wherever Helen lives.

After lunching under the walnut trees that shade the village of Imlil in the fertile Mizane Valley - and it was so good to run into my old friend Robbie Conder, who long ago departed the Home Counties for Imlil and has never once looked back - we trekked a few hours more before reaching our next base at Aroumd. All around us were the peaks that stand, almost in defensive formation, in front of Mount Toubkal. In fact, so well is Toubkal defended, we could see not so much as a bit of it.

It would be two days more before we glimpsed Toubkal. Two days in which to hike to base camp, two days to turn pudgy suburban bodies into sinewy climbing machines, two days to find ourselves at least one receptacle that might reasonably pass muster for a toilet, or if not a toilet, then at the very least a hole in the ground with a bit of space to take the job on.

We found it at the Neltner Refuge, splendidly and spotlessly run by the Club Alpine Francais, last stopping off point before the final ascent, and home to a production line of toilets, *real* toilets, the sit-down variety, paper and all. It was like manna from heaven. OK, the paper was covered in newsprint and narrative - I think it was Climbers' Weekly, or possibly a Moslem periodical called *What Veil Magazine* - but it was soft, pliable and thoroughly absorbent, and just to gaze on this confection of porcelain and paper was to realise how the Children of Israel must have felt when Moses brought forth water from the rock, or indeed how your average Leeds United footballer must feel when found not guilty of racially motivated assault, affray and grievous bodily harm. It was a miracle. After such joy unconfined, falling short on the way to the top of Toubkal simply was not an option.

And so it was that Brahim-Who-Shall-Be-Known-As-Brian saw fit once again to have us emerge barely four hours into the new day, and then to trample loose scree even looser on our way to the summit. It's all uphill on Toubkal. Not even the occasional stretch of level ground to lend a bit of respite. Instead, a 4,000 foot stretch up slippery scree, the kind that has you sliding back down on yourself with soul-destroying monotony. Forward three, slide back two, forward two, slide back one, forward one, catch your breath, forward three, so it goes. God it's relentless. The words 'glutton' and 'punishment' come to mind. So, too, the words 'what the fuck do I need this for at my time of life!?'

And yet, the longer I climbed, and the harder I pushed, the stronger I felt. Can you figure that? We're talking a crack-of-dawn assault on a genuinely tough peak, a one-in-two gradient the whole way, surfing through and finally piercing the early morning cloud-line on a wave of adrenaline and derring-do, and by the time the summit was in view, just before the final ridge, I felt there was little my slender frame couldn't endure, short of out-sculling Steve Redgrave down on Sydney Harbour.

Don't get the idea this kind of climbing is enjoyable. Sometimes it is. Climbing can be a truly inspirational experience, and there's nothing like a prolonged stretch of seriously tricky terrain to find out heaps more about yourself than you ever knew. But mostly it's a hard bloody slog. The enjoyment, the real enjoyment, lies in the achievement, and the achievement is hitting the top, drawing a long, deep breath, and for the first time in four hours - four mostly dark hours during which your eyes hardly even once venture from your feet - looking up from the ground and allowing your circular vision to drink in every last drop of panorama. The surroundings are majestic. They always are when you're this high up. But on Toubkal they really are something special, and I just stood and savoured the summit in quiet contemplation, my apparent nonchalance a flimsy mask for my huge sense of well-being. It's always that way with me and mountains.

We each descended at our own pace. Such is the reward of a successful climb. The pressure is off and you come back down as you please. Some race down, some amble, Bazza doubtless found his downward path somewhat wind-assisted, and some, like me, are oblivious to anything, or anyone, else for the next eight hours.

Actually, all of us were like that, content to bask in a quiet, leisurely descent. All except Andrew, that is. Andrew was our group's mountain-man, macho-man, and quite possibly five-times-a-night-and-not-come-up-for-air-man. Andrew's mission was to get everywhere first. Lunch, dinner, base camp, top of the mountain, bottom of the mountain, and all points between and beyond, toilets included. Andrew it was who described the final ascent as "a bit of a jog, no more challenging than Snowdon", though whether he meant the mountain or the lord is anyone's guess.

So it was with no small sense of schadenfreude that I watched Andrew run down Toubkal like a demented ferret on Benzedrine, hit a boulder with the full force of his considerable 14 stone, wince as his right knee stiffened and swelled like an extremely stiff and swollen thing, before hobbling back to Aroumd looking uncannily like Douglas Bader at a skateboard regatta. Poetic justice? I wouldn't be that mean. Bloody funny? You bet. There'd be some serious dining out on this one when I fetched up the next day for some serious rest-and-relaxation in Marrakech.

⁂

Ah, Marrakech, the perfect antedote to anything, any time, particularly Dar Moha Al Madina, the 19th century riad that once was the home of Pierre Balmain. With its cloistered garden, billowing palms, hanging bananas, and mosaic swimming pool, it was hard to believe I was in the heart of the Medina, the old walled city of Marrakech. It felt for all the world as though I was way out in the back of beyond, back in the foothills of the High Atlas perhaps, or amid the olive trees and farmland of Ouirgane.

But a climb to the riad's roof terrace soon put me right, the palaces and mosques of Marrakech opening up before me in living colour, the colour being pink, a hue which seems to cover every last inch of this remarkable city. Pink roads, pink walls, pink roofs, pink mosques, so pink, in fact, that Lady Penelope from Thunderbirds could drive her Cadillac through the heart of the city in perfect camouflage.

I was in Marrakech with my pal David, who had flown in to greet me off my climb and to confer on me - in the absence of my wife and kids who, unbeknownst to me, were planning an elaborate subterfuge of a birthday bash for me back in Blighty - the last rites of my forties. We had the riad all to ourselves, which is pretty much

how you book these atmospheric old town houses. And how we basked in the serenity of the place. No phone, no fax, no papers, no e-mail, the woes of the world held blissfully at bay.

Marrakech, though, is peaceful only on the inside. Open the door and you step out into a city of joyous energy - raucous and frenetic, vibrant and enormous fun, with a definite post-hippy-flowers-in-your-hair-sweet-smell-in-the-air vibe. Never mind about Clinton smoking but not inhaling. In Marrakech you can inhale without anything ever passing your lips and still get stupidly happy.

The pulsating heartbeat of the city is the Djemaa El Fna, the sprawling expanse of downtown tarmac that morphs at dusk from a grand prix circuit of taxis, scooters, horse drawn carriages and hundreds of misguided pedestrians, into a tidal wave of jugglers, balancers, acrobats, magicians, soothsayers, storytellers, snake charmers, sword swallowers....and hundreds more pedestrians, less misguided this time, as vehicles make way for a myriad street performers.

In the twinkling of an eye all transport evacuates the scene, as al fresco eateries set up all around the perimeter of the square, battalions of trestle tables armed and ready to feed shishlik, tajine and a score-and-more varieties of couscous to the hordes of hungry revellers. I don't know how many people converge on the Djemaa at night, but dress them all in red and white and you could call the place Old Trafford. By day the Djemaa is a sight to behold. By night it is truly awesome.

David and I gloried in this unique spectacle from various vantage points, mostly of the rooftop café variety, where the mint tea flows like Tetley's on a wet Wisbech Wednesday. From the Café Argana we gazed across the Djemaa to the ceramic inlaid minaret of the Koutoubia. From Café El Badi we sat eyeballing a family of kamikaze storks who had set up home on a quite absurdly narrow ledge atop the Royal Palace walls. I've had some pretty surreal experiences on my travels, but engaging in some sort of bizarre stare-out contest, glass of tea in hand, with a furry great black and white thing fifty feet above Marrakech is, I'm prepared to wager, as daft as it gets.

Even more surreal - and brave, let me tell you - is knocking back Whiskey Marocain (as the locals call mint tea) when I should have been making serious inroads into my daughter's shopping list. Lucy knows Marrakech to the last stall at closing time, and she had no trouble identifying which souk would provide what merchandise.

Thus was I to work my way from Souk Btana (sheepskin slippers) to Souk des Babouche (pointy pink slippers) via Souk des Bijoutiers (amber necklace), Souk

Cherratin (double-stitched, floral-patterned shoulder bag) and Souk Smarine (some yashmak thingy that I felt decidedly odd asking for, though trying it on certainly broke the ice!)

Never, by the way, photograph a yashmak-bedecked Moroccan lady. Modesty still prevails in these parts and you'll be warned off with a hiss, a scowl, and a word or two about pestilence (and no, it is not a veiled threat; I don't do puns). If this implies the folk of Marrakech are unfriendly, nothing could be further from the truth. The locals are happy to help and eager to please, and they seem especially knowledgeable about the city's long and colourful Jewish history.

Marrakech's Jewish flavour, alas, is no longer quite so pungent as it once was. Not so very long ago there were 25,000 Jews in Marrakech. Today perhaps 500 remain. But wander through the Mellah, the old Jewish quarter beyond the Place des Ferblantiers, and ye shall find. The embers of a more heimesche time still hang over the Mellah, where the streets, enclosed and brooding, retain their distinctive and utterly beguiling air of days gone by.

Several small synagogues remain, though only a few still reverberate to the sound of prayer, and those that do are mighty hard to find, largely because they look like - and indeed are - private houses. But meander along these narrow lanes on a Friday evening and the odds are you'll spot a knitted yarmulka. A friendly word and you'll be welcomed with open arms to a true Moroccan Shabbat.

David and I did our Jewish bonding at the Riad Souika, owned by a one-time high-ranking Israeli army officer and tucked away at the end of a tiny passage right around from the Royal Palace in the Medina's Berrima sector. We were out of time at the Dar Moha Al Madina, and Riad Souika came available the very same day. We could not have been happier. Souika is a beguilingly characterful old house, from the fountain and lemon-tree in the inner-courtyard via the menorah-adorned salon all the way to the roof terrace from which I was able to look back in wonder at the mountains.

We didn't hang around the riad too long, though, preferring instead to soak up the rumpus on the streets. Noise starts early in Marrakech, four in the morning to be

exact. This is when the prodigiously vocal muezzin booms his first call to prayer across the city. This sets off the roosters, which sets off the dogs, which sets off the rumbling dust carts (collecting or delivering, it's hard to tell), which sets off...well, think "Chad Gad Ya", the Dada-esque Passover song that tells the tale of one horror triggering another, involving a bucket, a goat and the Angel of Death (don't even ask!). It's that kind of story. Better yet, think Joe Pesci, desperate for a night's sleep, in *My Cousin Vinny*. It's that kind of place.

But Marrakech would not be Marrakech without the prevailing din. It's a din which defines the old city. And you can forgive the city all manner of din when you stumble, as we did, on tiny, sun-drenched, almost magically silent backwaters like the tumbling, crumbling Rahba Kedima, where apothecary stalls dispense cochineal from earthenware saucers on the sidewalk, or the heroically ramshackle La Criee Berbere, where every last inch of pavement, railing, and corrugated tin roof is draped with exotic, kaleidoscopically patterned floor coverings, a sort of al fresco Allied Carpets.

Such is Marrakech. Dusty and colourful, boisterous yet oddly calming. A city that quite literally glows in the sun. A city that only the most reluctant of souls could fail to take into their hearts. Above all, a city with that enduring late-Sixties-early-Seventies vibe that recalls, each time I am there, the sounds of Santana, Hendrix and Joni Mitchell. It's like Woodstock in pink. All that was missing was my guitar, my love-beads, and the words to "Marrakech Express". Now where's my Crosby, Stills & Nash songbook...?

ℭℨ

# BREAKFAST IN THE BUSH

"It's the law of the land", said Susan. "There's a natural order out there and the eland doesn't rank very high". Maybe so; but it doesn't make watching a slender beast being torn apart by ravenous cheetahs any easier to bear. There's nothing like a safari for playing on your baser instincts.

## Eight great journeys

6 am in Kenya. We've just watched the sun rise over this far flung corner of the Masai Mara game reserve, the sound of silence gently nudged by the soft whooshing of flames as they impel the hot air balloon that drifts lazily by on the bottom rung of a cloudless sky. The tiredness of our dawn start has all but disappeared, eager anticipation being the perfect wake-up call.

Our jeep pulls up in a small clearing amid the semi-dense forestation that conceals who knows what. We'll find out soon enough. Right now, though, it is the open ground that grabs our attention. There, crouching low to the ground, is a young eland, an elegant, achingly beautiful gazelle-like creature. He's alive. Just. Hovering over him are two young cheetah cubs, about three-quarter grown, toying with him under the watchful gaze of their mother.

The cheetahs pat the eland on his rump, let him loose to run a bit, then rein him in, barely tapping the reserves of their Olympian speed. It looks like play, a game of tag perhaps, or grandmother's footsteps, the eland waiting his turn to creep up on the cheetahs. But no. The cheetahs' intentions are a touch less sporting. They are learning to kill. This is Tom and Jerry played out for real, only this time Jerry's got no mousehole to run to, nowhere to hide.

For some twenty minutes, an eternity to the terrified eland, he is teased and tormented before - I am sorry to be so blunt - being quite literally eaten alive, the prevailing silence rudely punctured by the sound of cracking limbs and greedy chomping. Like Joe Pesci being buried alive in *Casino*, death never came more slowly, nor with such casual brutality. And all this just three or four feet away from us.

I couldn't watch, and yet at the same time I couldn't not watch, my head buried by turn in my hands and my camera lens, the episode as compelling as it was distressing. This is what we've come to see, even if we didn't know it - a real life kill, if that's not a touch oxymoronic, the very stuff safaris are made of. It was awful and it was awesome, and worse, it was the most blatant act of voyeurism imaginable. Like Geraldine and Josephine watching Spats Colombo emptying his magazine into Toothpick Charlie and his cronies in *Some Like it Hot*, we've been witness to a gangland massacre.

"It's the law of the land", says Susan, ever the pragmatist and warmed by a shot or two of Courvoisieur. "There's a natural order out here and I'm afraid the eland

doesn't rank very high". My wife's wisdom offers scant solace, not least on seeing, once the eland was fully exposed, that he was a she and she was pregnant. I could have cried.

What could possibly follow this? Something gentle and graceful, perhaps. Please, God, something gentle and graceful, something soft and pink and fluffy and...alive. Does he listen? Not a bit of it. Instead, this being quite clearly Eat-A-Neighbour-Day in East Africa, a huddle of vultures appear, looking oddly like airborne bailiffs, swooping down and devouring so ravenously the remains of some or other wretched creature, all that is left visible to the naked eye is a shofar-like horn and a few bloodied limbs. Not nice. Very not nice.

John, our guide, is blessed with an eye keener than the keenest eagle, and within minutes he's driving us into a thicket so dense you could lose a block of flats in there. He's seen something. He cautions us to total silence, and all at once I know just why it is that David Attenborough is so given to those hushed whispery tones.

We open the roof of the jeep and poke out our heads, squinting hard to gain any kind of meaningful focus in the midst of all the gorse and bracken and general overhang that envelops us. We look this way and that, forward and back, up and down, with not the faintest idea of what it is John expects us to find. We shrug, we sigh, we tut-tut-tut. We've been led up a blind alley on the wildest of wild goose chases, plus we aren't even allowed to talk.

There's nothing. Tracker John has failed us. We might just as well....and then, Geronimo. All but beneath us, so close to our jeep we hadn't even thought to look, is a pride of lions - Mum, Dad and assorted cubs, all of them basking and preening, one of them on his back, legs akimbo, just crying out for tummy tickles. They're gorgeous. Soft and fluffy - OK, not pink, but definitely soft and fluffy, and graceful and gentle, extremely gentle. Were common sense not to prevail over impulsive temptation I'd be out of the jeep to playfully frolic with these handsome cats and their cuddly kittens. But I'm a pragmatist too, and I'd sooner eat chopped liver than be chopped liver.

We leave the lions to their siesta and head out across the plain, our 4-wheel drive scattering hundreds of lolloping wildebeest, hartebeest, zebras and hyenas. Goodness me, but the wildebeest is an odd lot. With equine body and long flowing beard he looks for all the world half horse, half rabbi, which I guess means he can gallop and deliver a sermon at the same time. (I was going to say canter, but never milk a good gag dry).

I've always wanted to see wildebeest, ever since Basil Fawlty, with one of his most devastating pieces of invective, assaulted a complaining Mrs. Richards, she who had no apparent view from her room, with the immortal words: "Well, what did you expect to see out of a Torquay hotel bedroom window? Sydney Opera House, perhaps? The Hanging Gardens of Babylon? Herds of wildebeest sweeping majestically across the plain?"

"Hey Dad", says my son Gideon, "where's the elephants then?" Where indeed, as for my part the elephants of the Masai Mara are the precise reason I'm here in the first place. This is what I lay awake thinking of the previous night, unable to sleep through the incessant bellowing of the hippos that shared our base at the Mara Buffalo Camp. And when I say sharing I mean sharing, for the Mara hippos, far from contenting themselves with a night in the water, fetch up instead on the lawn right outside, and I mean right outside, the intrepid vacationers' cabins. Hippos are huge. Believe me, you notice these things when you draw back the curtain at four in the morning, peek outside, and find yourself being eyeballed by eyeballs the size of woks.

We continue to bump and grind across the plain. More balloons float by on their airborne safari. They are not, for obvious reasons, allowed to land in the reserve, not without an armed ranger on hand. A jeep is OK. Jeep's can effect a speedy getaway if need be. Not so the humble hot air balloon. One did land recently, we were told, and the rest, as they say, is history, as indeed are the passengers, a couple of whom, it seems, provided some hungry carnivores with a first rate second course in this third world corner of civilization. Man in a basket, quite a meal.

Past warthog and baboon, jackal and rhino, we continue our tour of God's back yard. Lions feed on zebra, oblivious and with imperious disregard to our proximity, and that of our cameras, before slaking their thirst at the nearest watering hole. Lesser beasts queue as if by rote for the pickings, daring not to get involved while the lions are around. Vultures hover. They too know their place.

We continue further, mesmerized by the sheer scale of this, the very ultimate in live theatre. More cheetahs come into view, our wish for something cuddly once again granted, this time in the shape of the tiniest, fluffiest little cheetah kittens you ever saw. Three of them, picture postcard cute, stepping out behind their mum, shuffling through the dust, learning to walk, not yet killers, the very picture of wide-eyed innocence.

On we go, giraffe and bison bounding by in unlikely tandem, not unlike Jack Charlton and Vanessa Feltz. More wildebeest lollop and lope across our path, hyenas too, and rhinos, and gazelles, and monkeys down from the trees. It's a cavalcade of wildlife, a procession of exotic beings, a veritable royal variety performance on a thousand-and-four legs. It's a riot of colour and a riot of sound, honking and howling, hooting and hollering, until suddenly...silence once more. As suddenly as the landscape was thick with life, now there is nothing, just emptiness and space, as though every last beast of the Masai Mara has taken up the offer of eternal salvation among the goddess of plenty in return for instant migration.

We stop, look, listen. Then, with a silent grace and elegance that belies their size, a herd of elephants appear from nowhere, striding by in a way that suggests they've just watched *Jungle Book* and decided to stage a re-enactment for their own

amusement. How on earth do these immense creatures move so sedately and with such elegant poise? Nothing that big should be that dainty. It's like watching Oliver Hardy doing that little dance in *Way Out West.* All the elephants need are some gingham handkerchiefs to twirl above their heads and some lonesome pines to sing about.

On they go to the watering hole for their morning ablutions. On we go in search of whatever else is out there that we haven't yet seen, and surely to goodness there can't be much that we haven't yet seen. Our nerve ends are tingling, our cameras cocked and ready. And this is just day one of our safari.

We were lucky. Some people, I'm told, see lions, but not cheetahs. Others see rhino, but not elephants. And others see no big cats of any description, no rhino, no elephants, nothing much at all really, just the odd chimp or two and the ubiquitous herds of rabbinical horses. Us? We had the lot, no holds barred, finest piece of entertainment I ever saw. This was no B-movie, this was an Academy Award winner, worthy of every last statuette, and in the best tradition of the Oscars I'd like to thank John the Driver, my son the cameraman, my wife the pragmatist, Mum, Dad......

৪৪

# BELIZIAN DREAMS

Meet Katy, Belize's self-styled "professional Jew".
I'm Jewish too. But there's a difference between
me and Katy - a small difference, I'll grant you,
but a difference nonetheless. I grew up listening
to the music of Steely Dan, Katy grew up
*sleeping* with them.

## Eight great journeys

Belize is tiny. Look at it on the map - and if your map pre-dates the birth of punk music, it won't even say Belize, it'll say British Honduras - and you'll find a tiny sliver of land, barely bigger than Wales, shoehorned into Central America between Guatemala, the Yucatan Peninsula of Mexico, and the Caribbean. If it had decent roads - and for all of its many qualities Belize does not have one road you would call even modestly fast; it's like driving on lumpy blancmange - you could criss-cross the country, north to south, east to west, in well under a day and still have time for a drive-in movie, a tacos take-out from the local diner, and the second half of Big Creek Rovers versus Monkey River Wanderers. Trust me; it *is* tiny.

And yet, despite its postage-stamp size Belize manages to contain a perfectly stunning diversity of landscape, from the Mayan Mountains, through dense jungle, swampy creeks, and mountain pine ridge, to the translucent waters - an ocean you can see through right the way to the bottom - of the world's longest unbroken barrier reef.

The vibe is Caribbean, the national sport sleeping. "We don't need no national flag", the waiter at Belize City's Sooty Mermaid restaurant declared. "We just fly that ol' pillowcase". Belizians are almost terminally laid back, sometimes requiring a gentle prod to elicit some sort of response, or just to make sure they're alive and breathing.

Exactly how laid back I found out in the lobby of the city's Fort George Hotel down on the waterfront where, together with my wife and some time travelling partner Susan, I was stationed for my first night in this miniature land of mighty contrasts.

We were checking out of the hotel when an imposing looking guy walked in. Big lad. Bob Marley T-shirt, denim cargo shorts, shark-tooth necklace, CD discman looped through his belt, and a funky pair of Ray-Bans to die for. If he wasn't a rapper, then he'd certainly been a pretty tasty heavyweight in his day. This guy was seriously cool. "Good morning Mr. Prime Minister", the doorman said. God, that was impressive. The number one man in the land formerly painted pink on the Commonwealth map, and here he was, sitting down for breakfast in as much designer gear as you could shake a platinum-coated credit card at. No minder, no entourage, just his son and daughter and a mighty stack of hot-cakes and maple syrup.

Belize City may be the country's largest town - a third of Belize's 200,000 people live there - and it may also be the country's centre of commerce, such as it is, and heaven knows it's hard enough to imagine how the abacus ever made way for the calculator in this soporiphic corner of humanity. But it contrives also to be the only city I know whose airport seems somehow to have been cunningly fashioned from somebody's back garden.

We were at the airport to head east to the jungle, a way up in the Orange Walk District between the Rio Bravo and the Guatemalan border. This meant flying Air Tropic, a one-plane outfit whose owner and pilot, it is entirely possible, was a Mr. Tropic. He looked tired, his plane even more so, and it seemed a crying shame to bring either out of retirement. The plane, in fact - and it was a beaut, a real piece of work, a single-engine four seater effort that probably saw a lifetime's action and more in the last two World Wars - was downright reluctant to show any kind of reaction to all of Mr. Tropic's best efforts to get it started.

"It's a bit basic", he said, stretching understatement pretty much to the limit. "But we'll get there".

"Can I do something to help get this thing up?" I enquired, offering all the benefit of my zero experience or intelligence in these matters. "Jump leads, gaffer tape, Viagra?"

A quick tyre change and a wing-flap repair later we were ready for the off. Mr. Tropic's safety instructions were brief and commendably to-the-point. "Fasten your seat belts, take your feet off my seat, and place your faith in Jesus". I managed the first two. Be warned: When a pilot describes his own plane as "a bit basic", check him very closely for signs of irony.

☙

Well, the flight was great, uneventful in a positive way, and the landing at Gallon Jug Airstrip was little short of miraculous...for a 3-wheeler (it was originally four, but one wheel fell off over the jungle). This wasn't the kind of plane that has steps that fold down to the ground to assist your disembarkment. In fact Gallon Jug wasn't the kind of airstrip that has steps they can wheel to the plane. This was a job for upturned orange boxes, which I think gives you an idea how things are done in this part of the world.

We were met off the plane by a guy called Tom Harding, a grizzled, chisel-jawed giant of a man who wouldn't have looked out of place arguing the toss with Katherine Hepburn in *The African Queen*. Together we drove through the jungle, past swamps and creeks and bits of aircraft, to our lodge - *his* lodge - at Chan Chich, deep in the remotest heartland of nowhere. This place was not just off the beaten track, it was off the face of the Earth, a world away from the grimy semi-detached suburban mayhem we call civilization.

Tom showed us to our cabana and our hearts soared. It was an oasis of calm, like a ground-level tree-house, sheltered from the burning sun by a canopy of huge, billowing palm leaves, the silence punctuated only by the howling of monkeys, the clacking of toucans, and the growling of whatever your imagination allowed you to believe was out there, and quite possibly was.

We spent five days at Chan Chich, meandering through the jungle, sometimes on foot, sometimes on horseback, every so often scrambling up the grass-covered walls of a buried temple that once reverberated to the chants of ancient Mayans at prayer. And each day, as the sun went down, we would return to the lodge's wildlife blackboard, eagerly scribbling the names of freshly sighted fauna out there in the undergrowth and up among the rustling leaves and branches that parrots and marmots call home.

Tom is a fine host down at Chan Chich, and clearly at ease with his new remoteness from the big American city in which he once flew high as a captain of industry. He's one wildlife expert too.

"What's that?" I asked, as we sat out on the stoop beneath the stars.

"Kinky Jew", Tom replied.

"I shan't take that personally", I joked.

"That's kinkajou", he said, spelling it out for emphasis. "K-I-N-K-A-J-O-U. Kinkajou. A noisy skunk-like creature that comes out at night".

I still didn't take it personally.

Animal sightings were plentiful and spectacular at Chan Chich. All the usual suspects were there, and more besides. Ant eaters, coti mundi, bat falcons, keel-billed toucans, tiny orange-breasted falcons, enormous harpy eagles, gaily coloured tocororo birds flown all the way south-west from Cuba, electric-blue morpho butterflies, armies of leaf-cutter ants, batallions of monkeys, mandrills and other primates of every description, big primates, little primates, in-between primates, and cockroaches the size of football boots, right down to the moulded studs.

Nothing, though, had me purring quite like my big cat sighting. Not a *big* big cat, but a small big cat. Ocelot. Not quite a jaguar, hardly even the old-shape 16-valve Saab of the feline fraternity. But it was plenty big enough for me to dine out on, especially as there was barely a paw's length between us, the more so as, apparently, it was the first ocelot sighting for close on six months. It was over very quickly. I saw *it, it* saw me, *it* pissed off to anonymity. Seven seconds. That's all it takes to be David Attenborough.

Curious that big cats don't scare me, because spiders most definitely do. At least, they *did* until I took a night walk in the jungle at Chan Chich. OK, I'll admit, I'm still a big baby when it comes to spotting spiders scuttling across the kitchen floor, or worse yet, in the bath, at the exact same moment as I've managed to lodge my big toe up and inside the cold tap, thus rendering myself quite unable to effect a speedy getaway.

But out in the open I punch my true weight, and teasing a furry great, hairy-legged, wok-sized tarantula out of its hidey-hole with a twig, dimming my torch so as to be illuminated by its piercing red eyes, lifted me to new levels of bravery. In fact, if the tarantula had popped out of his hidey-hole to greet me together with his entire family and entourage of friends and neighbours from the hidey-holes up and down the road, I do believe I'd have stood my ground, unhesitatingly and unflinchingly, quite possibly stooping to ground level for closer inspection.

Back in our cabana there was a spider. I slept outside on the hammock.

&#8478;

Onwards to Chaa Creek Cottages, where Lucy and Mick Fleming - she from New Jersey, he from Tunbridge Wells - have created an exquisite wonderland, carving out of the hillside a haven of peace and tranquility. From luxurious cabanas for the

pampered travel writer to simple log cabins for the shallow-of-pocket, Lucy and Mick cater for everyone, even those in search of a good old-fashioned rub down at their heavenly spa, all soothing music, smouldering incense, and herbal linen and seaweed wraps.

Refreshed and replenished after a morning's massage, I commandeered a boat on the banks of the creek and canoed down river to the town of San Ignacio. Accompanied only by Susan, a flock of flapping green parrots, and a flight of brilliant blue kingfishers that seemed to guide our way, I rowed this beguiling course of the Macal River, through gently nudging rapids, past tumbledown waterfront shacks-on-stilts, with not another canoe, or row-boat of any kind, in sight. We had the whole river to ourselves. It was as though the entire world had somehow backed off and retired graciously to allow us our afternoon of peace and solitude.

Once at San Ignacio Susan played to type - her type being sensible, well-balanced, normal - and hitched a ride back to Chaa Creek in Mick's comfy new Land Rover, which his driver had brought to town just for that purpose. Me? Not so sensible. I hauled a mountain bike off the roof of the Land Rover and proceeded to cycle back. Ten miles as the parrots fly, fifteen by road, uphill all the way.

This is something I've yet to figure out, a true geological conundrum. Everywhere in Belize is uphill. Even the level bits have a gradient. Pop yourself on a bike in Belize's rolling interior and you find yourself exercising muscles you never knew you had. I'd need a mathematician, or at the very least my accountant, to work out just how many calories I kicked off from San Ignacio to Chaa Creek. And with tarmac yet to reach this corner of the Americas, I arrived back at the lodge, wild-eyed and half-crazed, like the Lone Biker of the Apocalypse with a very sore bottom.

I submitted myself to the Flemings' daughter, Bryony, for another massage. I had some kinks needed ironing out, and an hour's aromatherapy, with the soothing accompaniment of swirling tablas and mandolins, seemed just the ticket and the perfect preparation for the rigours of the night.

Sundown in the moody, dimly-lit bar at Chaa Creek was tale-swapping time. Most of us told tales of derring-do on the High Seas and the High Sierra, in some cases Borneo and Patagonia, in others Tierra del Fuego and the Cape of Good Hope, and in my case Brighton and Bournemouth, which is fair enough since that's where my kids live at their respective universities. My new friend Katy, on the other hand, went one better, several better in fact. She told us, in graphic, lurid and thoroughly entertaining detail, every last person she'd slept with back in her wild years of loft dwelling in her native Manhattan, which for the main part, and for reasons best known to herself, appeared to be Jewish musicians.

Let me fill in the spaces for you. Belize has just two resident Jews that anyone knows of (though many more, I'm sure, will come tumbling out the closet once this book hits the streets of Central America). 200,000 people, 2 Jews. That means one one-hundred-thousandth of Belize is officially Jewish. Proportionately speaking that's the equivalent to the number of brain cells per square centimetre in George W. Bush's head.

One of those Jews is Katy. She is the self-styled "professional Jew of the Mayan Mountains", offering Yiddishisms, Old Country wisdom and a heaving bosom to anyone passing through with a wish to encounter "Jewish Belize", which of course doesn't exist, other than in Katy's anecdotes, and those of Belize's other resident Jew who I was yet to meet.

"Yeah…I did a few rock stars", Katy drawled in a voice that sounded curiously like Jerry Seinfeld on acid. "Jew-boy rock stars, too. Decades on my back and never once a goy. Never forget your roots, boy". Great. I was getting a lesson in music and morality from a shag-happy yenta who was destined, in the immortal words of Edmund Blackadder, to be buried in a Y-shaped coffin.

This was worth hearing, even if it took a bottle or two of deep red wine to keep pace with the kind of love life that most White House interns during the Clinton administration could only dream of. Not only, it transpires, did this good lady promote the legendary Steely Dan back in their pomp, but she actually shared her apartment with Walter Becker. One of my all-time rock-and-roll heroes, the man whose guitar licks on "Reelin' In The Years" and "Babylon Sisters" still sends goose bumps down my spine, and I passed time, and damn near passed out, with the woman who smoothed his duvet.

I was impressed. I was more than impressed; I was speechless. Her stories were so outrageous there was no way they weren't true, and when she told me who the Dan's seminal album "Katy Lied" was named for it all made perfect sense, and I knew at once I was in the presence of a kindred spirit, a goddess, the high priestess of Judeo-rock-and-roll fornication.

Together we tiptoed into the wee small hours dissecting, dissembling and disembowelling the most obscure of Steely Dan's lyrics, from "Kid Charlemagne" to "Pretzel Logic", until every last song made sense, even "Haitian Divorce", which has had academics, philosophers and coke-heads pulling their hair out since the dawn of civilization. We worked them out, Katy and me, no problem. A lifetime's work in five alcohol-fuelled hours. Formal education? Who needs it?

ଔ

From Chaa Creek we took a day out in Guatemala to explore the extraordinary lost temples of Tikal, a fabulous confection of excavated splendour, the sheer scale of which is quite overwhelming. But first we had a border to cross close to the scabby little hick town of Benque Viejo Del Carmen, a place whose name is considerably more extensive than its 'attractions' which, principally, are a quite dazzling array of insects and assorted other pestilence, exceeded only by those on offer just across the border at the heroically dusty town of Melchor de Mencos.

This entailed negotiating, and negotiating *with,* the Guatemalan border police and the ubiquitous roaming gangs of calamitously amateurish armed robbers - armed for the most part with extreme Spanish sarcasm - and frankly it is only the uniforms of the former that renders them in any way distinguishable from the latter. Either will whisk you across the border and into their Dodge City of a country faster than the seemingly, if not officially, regulation four hours, just so long as you "see them alright". The contrast beween the two countries is marked, almost exaggeratedly so. Imagine crossing, especially by train, from the fastidious order of Switzerland into the inspired lunacy of Italy. Belize into Guatemala is not all that different.

Of course, you can always avoid these shenanigans by flying across the border from Belize City to the cobbled and actually rather atmospheric old town of Flores, which is beautifully sited on a small island in the middle of Lake Peten Itza. In fact, the causeway that connects Flores to the rest of Guatemala doubles as the airstrip's runway. It's more expensive than hitching the San Ignacio bus across the border, but what with the tips, bribes and blood money you'll undoubtedly part with at the land border crossing, it's six of one, half a dozen of the other. Either way Tikal offers an unforgettable day out, and the border crossing, whichever way you do it, is all part of the fun.

The atmosphere at Tikal is spellbinding, and it is impossible not to be impressed at the sight of these immense temples, which in effect are steep-sided pyramids, some with rather unevocative names like Complex Q and Complex R, though North Acropolis and Central Acropolis at least make an effort at evocation with the word Acropolis. The pyramids are vast - some of them rise 200 feet above the forested canopy towards the sky - and the Jaguar Temple in particular just takes the breath away, its soaring peak silhouetted against the brilliant reds and yellows of the toucans that squabble for space on the overhanging branches. What an incredible sight.

Needless to say I shinned my way up and down every last one of the pyramids, with their ludicrously steep Inca-like steps, praying to the God of photography that Susan's zoom lens would capture those heroic moments for posterity. With a hundred or so metres between us, and Susan rooted to ground level along the somewhat ingloriously named Tozzer Causeway, it was in all senses a long shot. But she managed in great style and, our day at Tikal done, we moved on out of Guatemala with a packful of finished film and a skinful of authentic ingrained Guatemalan dust.

❦

# BELIZIAN DREAMS

Credit where it's due, Susan's pretty nifty with a camera. Mind you, she's no Francis Ford Coppola. I know this for a fact. I've seen all of Coppola's movies, both my kids scrutinised his work for their 'A' level film studies, and I've now stayed in his home - one of them anyway - the breathtaking Blanceneaux Lodge way up in the clear air of the Mountain Pine Ridge.

I'd like to say I met the man. I spent weeks rehearsing the line "they killed my boy Sonny" with a satsuma lodged in each cheek. I've even managed to work the word "apocalypse" into this story at every turn without seriously losing context. But he never showed. Oh, there was plenty of Coppolaptic presence to keep me amused, from the *Rumble Fish* and *Godfather* posters on the walls of our cabana to the actual ceiling fan that cooled Martin Sheen in those opening shots of *Apocalypse Now*. But it's not the same, not for a sad old film buff like me.

You see, I'm am absolute anorak when it comes to movies, and short of meeting Joel and Ethan Coen and asking them to thank their mum and dad on my behalf for creating the creators of *Miller's Crossing* and *The Big Lebowski*, I guess meeting F.F. Coppola and spluttering out the words: "Apocalypse Now....unreal, man!" would just about do it for me.

Still, he wasn't there, so I went caving instead down on Barton Creek. Drifting deeper and deeper into the cave, the darkness punctuated only by the spear-like shafts of light from the hair's-breadth overhead fissures, the beam of our headlamps provided all the invitation needed for the local fruit bats to use our heads as some kind of target practice. With this frenzied aerial assault - really, it was very Hitchcockian, like The Birds, only without the manic pecking on the phone box and Tippi Hedren trying to look sexy in a headscarf - we canoed to the point of no return in a very dark and spooky place.

The options were simple - row back or get out the boat. Gilberto, our guide in the creek, asked us if we fancied hopping out the canoe for a scramble up the cave's slimy walls, dodging stalagmites and stalactites as we went. Susan didn't. She's sensible, remember? Me? I said yes. It seemed like a good idea at the time.

Barefoot, intrepid, and very very silly, I got to the top and was greeted warmly by Susan, Gilberto, and Mike Booger, an immense Fozzie Bear of a man who traded computing in Ontario for cave-owning in Barton Creek. Five years and 300 acres of land later Mike's a happy landlord, and with neighbours and tenants ranging from

Mayans to Mestizos, via pockets of Amish-like, denim-clad, buggy-driving Mennonite communities, Mike's drinking buddies are nothing if not diverse.

I number my few days at Blanceneaux among the most peaceful I've known. Swaying lazily in the hammock outside our cabana, the sound of water rippling, sometimes thundering, from the waterfall just a few steps away, I gave silent thanks to the bountiful Mr. Coppolla for providing us with such idyllic and heavenly surroundings. And this from the man who placed the Vatican in the hands of the mafia and a severed head on the lap of Martin Sheen.

☙

From 'Coppolodge' we headed to the coast, along the endearingly named Hummingbird Highway, passed settlements called Middlesex, Tea Kettle, and Over-The-Top. Guide books describe the Hummingbird Highway as one of the best roads in Belize. This is a little like describing "Maggie May" as one of the best tunes in the Rod Stewart songbook; the competition ain't exactly great. But who needs to bust through the speed limit in such scenic surroundings? These are roads on which to amble at 20 miles an hour, and never mind that you have to anyway on account of the monumentally crap surface.

Over looping hills, through lush green forest, and past the achingly gorgeous, and gorgeously named, Five Blues Lake National Park, we drove, until finally we arrived at Jaguar Reef Lodge, an enticing, loosely-affiliated collection of white-washed, thatched cabanas strewn almost as an afterthought along the beach just south of the tiny fishing village of Hopkins.

I like to think I know a good beach when I see one - though heaven knows I'll take anything after years of scuffing my toes on Brighton's pebbled floor - and Jaguar Reef is little short of sensational. Miles of soft, deep, golden sand and nothing but the Caribbean between us and the cayes - pronounced keys - the micro-miniscule islets that dot the horizon and line the barrier reef way out at sea on route to the West Indies. This is snorkelling country, where you boat out to a turquoise wonderland, chuck yourself overboard, and watch the greatest sub-aqua show on Earth.

Our speedboat darted this way and that, slowing just enough for us to dive into a rainbow of colour a few hundred metres short of the tiniest desert island you ever saw. It was called Tobacco Caye and it was barely 200 metres square if it was an inch. One middling sized wave - that's all it would take to wash the island clean away.

Just the names of the cayes are enough to make you weep with joy. Black Adore Caye, Half Moon Caye, Hunting Caye, Middle Long Caye, Southern Long Caye, Wild Cane Caye, Caye Caulker, Big Caye Bokel. They sound so enticing, so inviting, something in their names drawing you magnetically to their coral fringes in much the same way Pratts Bottom draws you southwards to Kent in the Garden of England.

Face down on the surface of the ocean we found ourselves eyeballed by angel fish, parrot fish, barracuda, stingrays, and sharks of varying sizes and even more shades of black. I'm the worlds worst swimmer; that much is statistically factual and on the record. But there was no way on Earth you'd get me out of that water. It was strange, it was beautiful, it was like nothing I'd ever seen on or off dry land, a cinematic underworld that even Coppolla would be hard pushed to create. And for all that it was hard not to feel I was somehow intruding on someone else's territory; not just the creatures of the deep, but the handful of people too who had somehow made their home not just in Belize, but on a micro-patch of sand miles out at sea.

Belize, together with its desert islands, is rich in people who came for vacation and never went home, except perhaps to sell up and get a divorce. Mike Booger and Tom Harding are perfect examples. For Jennifer Hall, now residing on a 300 metre by 300 metre carpet of sand called South Water Caye, the transition 15 years ago from Bigtown USA - technology, pollution, husband - to a dot on the map so tiny it isn't even *on* the map, was apparently seamless.

Her life shared only with the odd passing snorkeller, the resident pelican population, and the students who visit her pioneering ecology centre, Jennifer is, I believe, as content a soul as I have ever met. I am envious and admiring in equal measure, and if I could find a kosher deli and twenty-one other guys to play football with, I do believe I could happily set up home on South Water Caye.

I met Belize Jew Number Two at our last stop, The Inn at Robert's Grove. Named after its owner and creator, Robert Frackman, the Inn is perched at the tip of the Placencia Peninsula, a slender neck of land approached via pine forest and banana plantations from a dirt road due east of the euphemistically named Southern Highway, the word 'highway' transgressing all manner of statute concerning misrepresentation.

Placencia itself is a small fishing village and is beyond all shadow of doubt one of the most wonderful places I've ever washed up. Robert's Grove goes one step further. It *is* Heaven on Earth, pure and simple, shaded by palm trees and cooled by the gentle sea breeze, the ocean waves lapping perilously close to your feet *even* when you're indoors. This is where land and sea have no barrier, and for five criminally hedonistic days my consciousness was invaded by nothing more than the periodic twinge of regret that this journey would soon be over.

Robert's Grove was the perfect place for Susan and me to end our pitifully short stay in this extraordinary little country, and Robert Frackman was the perfect host for our final few days. Avuncular and heimesche, with more than a passing resemblance to Uncle Junior from *The Sopranos*, Frackman re-visits his ethnic roots each and every Passover, hosting a traditional Seder service and meal - imported matzas, Hebrew National sausages, and all - out on the beach, under the stars, exactly, I would like to believe, as God intended.

Frackman's laid-back, pioneering spirit - you just know he'd run his own beach-front kibbutz were he to set up in Israel - is echoed everywhere you go in Belize, the new-settler breeze washing over you like spring water in the desert. The country is unhurried and unspoiled, as though defiantly rooted in a time warp, little having changed since it was a tiny splash of pink on the old colonnial atlas, a time when John The Bakerman, still a fixture in Placencia, first started baking his Creole breads and buns for the locals. A time also when Olga - no-one, it seems, in all of Belize has ever known her surname - set up Olga's Store, store meaning shack, and no shack being quite so

welcoming as Dis'n'Dat, with it dazzling range of clearly non-perishable foods, some of which are said even to pre-date Belize's independence from the British Empire several decades ago.

Most unchanged of all is the Cozy Corner, just along the strip from the Pickled Parrot Bar & Grill, and still, as it always has been, the most iconic and atmospheric of Placencia's beach bars, a place where bandana-clad local ex-pats gather at sundown, and pretty much most other times too, over a rum punch to swap tales of substance-fuelled excess back in Tallulah Bankhead City, or Viagra Heights South Dakota, or whatever hillbilly town they descended from.

With its green awning, ageing hippies, and an oddly Wild West kind of a vibe, all it needed, aside from The Doors and Janis Joplin blasting out of the ancient speakers at each corner of the tarpaulin, was Dennis Hopper propping up the bar, half-a-dozen cameras slung around his neck, muttering: "This is one crazy fucking trip, man", to complete the illusion that we had somehow stumbled onto the set of *Apocalypse Now*.

I felt gloriously removed from reality and very much at home. And when my sunburnt feet were used as some sort of towpath by a pair of high-velocity, spiny-tailed iguanas, I knew at once, blissfully and joyfully, how far - how very, very far - I'd strayed from the real world, and how very little I wanted to return.

༄

# TROUBLE IN PARADISE

My emotions are confused at the best of times. Israel, though, grabs them by the scruff, shakes them for all they're worth, before turning them into so much scrambled egg. The country is an extension of the Jewish family, and like all families, Jewish or otherwise, Israel upsets, infuriates and is riddled with imperfections. But it's still family.

## Eight great journeys

I have travelled to Israel some twenty, perhaps thirty, times since I first did what is now referred to in Jewish youth circles as "The Israel Experience" on leaving school. I even had a home in Jerusalem from 1986 to 1990, which I subsequently sold for reasons ranging from ideological through quasi-political via downright confusing. Israel does this to you. It stirs an awful lot of feelings and emotions, the more so the closer you hold the country to your heart.

I have holidayed in Israel, visited friends and family in Israel, worked on kibbutz in Israel, run the 100 and 200 metres for my country in Israel (in the 4-yearly Maccabiah Games a.k.a. the Jewish Olympics), *lived* in Israel...heck, I even played soccer for my country in Israel just a few short months ago as part of a somewhat creaky British Masters (a.k.a. veterans) football team.

This last visit, for the dual purposes of soccer and solidarity, was beyond all shadow of doubt my most positive and uplifting Israel experience on record, and I say this notwithstanding the ghost town Israel has now become, and for reasons on which I need hardly elaborate, in terms of tourism.

It was a privilege to visit the Armored Corps Museum at Latrun, the many and various Jewish National Fund projects both in the desert and in the cities, the Nitzana youth village and educational community down in the Negev alongside the Egyptian border, the Tel Hashomer Hospital in Tel Aviv (you gain all kinds of perspective on meeting victims of terrorism), and above all the Beit Uri complex in Afula, where the severely mentally and physically handicapped are looked after with the kind of compassion and tenderness that makes me so proud to be a Jew. And as if this weren't enough, we played football too...and lost. (A touch more success on the soccer field - now *there* would be a story!)

But it was my last-but-one visit to Israel, a few months earlier in 2002, that really stirred me up. I hope on reading this you will understand why. And I hope you will understand too how easy it is for abnormal circumstances to cause such radical shifts in personal perception and political bias as in those of my friends out there, the vast majority of whom, like me, are some way 'left of centre', but who sometimes feel the pull of the right, usually when attending the funeral of a neighbour or friend...or child.

# TROUBLE IN PARADISE

## DAY ONE...

Driving from Ben Gurion up to Jerusalem was emotional - very, *very* emotional - a wellspring of feelings from nostalgia to regret, sadness to hope, filling my head and both warming and cooling my heart. It was three-and-a-half years since I was last here - the longest I have ever been in all of my adult life between visits to my spiritual homeland - 12 years since I sold my flat with a view across the once peaceful Arab hills and village of Sur Bahar, and a lifetime and more since I first let Israel stampede across my consciousness and into my soul.

I was at Mevasseret Zion - the name alone, Prophecy of Zion, is so evocative - within a half hour or so, and there was my old mate Raymond to welcome me, as he always does, with a brotherly hug and kiss as though I were indeed the brother he never had.

The afternoon had all but faded and we had barely time to light the Shabbat candles, make Kiddush, and watch the sun set over the hills of Abu Ghosh before heading off for a dinner date down in the old artists' colony of Ein Kerem with Raymond's friends Andie and Steve.

A feisty English couple who originate from the decidedly unfeisty suburb of East Barnet, Andie and Steve are as secular as any secular Jews can be, making all the more stark the contrast between themselves and their youngest son, who has recently embraced Hassidism with all the piety and zeal of the truly impressionable (though fair play to him for returning to the bosom of the ritually-challenged family to share in Kabbalat Shabbat).

The whole family was there. Daughters, boyfriends, husbands, remoter issue, and their-son-the-new-Hassid and his b'sheitled wife who, at first glance, I thought was sitting, for some reason best known to herself, with a beaver on her head.

It was a fun evening, laid back, perfectly relaxed, the conversation animated and challenging (as it always is in Israel), and with the distinct feeling that Andie and Steve were my old friends too. And how lovely to share Shabbat in such a characterful old house, all exposed stonework and open beams, and with rampaging foliage spilling its all from every vestibule and patio into the house, around the walls and ceilings, and very nearly onto the dinner table.

Israel's troubles seemed a million miles away.

## DAY TWO...

In short, the perfect Shabbat.

Up late, a walk with Raymond, Raymond's boy Nadav, and Snowy the dog (who is brown, by the way, so why he's called Snowy is anyone's guess) through the hills that drop away from Raymond's house; lunch in the garden - can you imagine such a thing in January? - followed by a shluf on the recliner under a truly unseasonal burst of warm sunshine. And then, to cap it all, Havdalah, the traditional adieu to Shabbat with the burning of the crinkly blue-and-white candle, and the English football results, just like the old days, the results remaining a constant of my Saturday afternoons, Havdalah having fallen by the wayside since I first started watching Luton all those years ago.

In the evening I went to Allan and Roberta, friends from further back even than Raymond and the absent Judith, who was on a Florida freebie with her folks. Allan was adamant I come this evening since, as fate would have it, he was throwing a little birthday bash for an old friend of the both of us...in his case friend, in my case girlfriend, or at least she would have been had she ever - once would have sufficed - allowed me beyond first base. We're talking Daniella, the most mysterious and elusive adolescent female ever to emerge from the posh end of Finchley Central.

It was good to see her after longer - far, far longer - than I care to remember, and still every bit as beguilingly attractive as ever, in that Elaine-from-Seinfeld kind of a way. Also there was Evelyn, whose underwear I had been no less keen to occupy all those years ago, and whose stubborn reluctance to play ball was no less profound than Daniella's. I didn't take it personally, not in either instance. Instead I asked each of them if perhaps they had a younger sister I might get lucky with. They did. I didn't.

It was a nice evening. Howie and Elaine, other old friends and the fastest talking Canadians you ever met, were there, plus some others I'd never met, and so too Daniel, Allan and Roberta's son, who is now quite indistinguishable from the tank he probably once commanded. Big, strong lad. Looks uncannily like my Gideon, with that broad, squat, beer barrel of a chest, and close-cropped chestnut hair. I wonder if he and Gids are in any way related. Just a thought.

## DAY THREE...

It's a sad thing to see such a big, glamorous, state-of-the-art and magically located new hotel stand forlornly in a sorry state of stark near-emptiness, many of its floors closed off and shut down. It's like that for so many of Jerusalem's hotels, none more so, it seems, than the beautiful David Citadel Hotel just down from the King David Hotel on the edge of Mamilla, with views to die for across the walls of the Old City.

## TROUBLE IN PARADISE

I went there early morning to use their gym. There were just four of us there. Me, a personal trainer, the guy he was training, and the guy-he-was-training's bodyguard. I recognized the guy straight off. Who wouldn't? Famous, this guy. Very famous indeed. I didn't let on though. I thought I'd engage him in a little gym chat and play the naïve country boy, perhaps tease out his sense of humour, something I don't recall ever seeing him display in all the times I'd caught his 'act'.

"You're on TV, aren't you", I said. "Comedian, chat shows, that sort of thing". I kept a commendably straight face. So did he.
"Not a comedian", he said.
"Singer?" I ventured
"Not a singer", he said. "But I have been on television once or twice".

I think he smiled as he said this. Which was nice; for it's usually something of a dark scowl you see on the face of Binyamin Netanyahu. I'd love to have discussed the state of the nation and other such stuff with him. But I know my place, so we discussed instead the comparative merits of the bench press and the lateral pull-down, and even swapped notes about tight hamstrings, strained quadriceps and nutrition supplements. Even weightier matters, some might say.

My workout done I made for the Hillel Espresso Bar on Hillel Street for a late breakfast and a journal update, before heading down King George Street for a piece of pizza and a slice of solidarity. For it was only solidarity - together, perhaps, with the misplaced notion that lightning never strikes the same place twice - that led me to Jerusalem's downtown Sbarro Pizza Parlour so soon after a Palestinian suicide bomber had visited upon it such scenes of unspeakable carnage and horror.

Now you may say I should know better, but truly you don't expect a casual stroll to metamorphose without a second's notice into genocide, not even on the streets of west Jerusalem, and not even as a seasoned visitor to Israel's capital city. You know it happens to others, it's an ever-present item of world news; but you never think it might happen to you.

I had barely one foot through the restaurant's front door when an unholy blast blew me clean off my feet and back into the street. Miraculously I wasn't hurt, the full force of the blast being borne by those around me. I had a few surface cuts, some glass fragments needed picking out of my shaven head, but that was it. Dusty, but pretty much unscathed. Others were not so lucky. Many others, it transpired, as scores, perhaps even hundreds, of people were mangled, maimed and, in some cases, killed by the latest suicide bomb to hit Israel. And God knows how many more will have died before these words have hit the printed page.

My instinct for self-preservation flew out the window as I dusted myself down and reached for my note-book, my camera and my press card. I crunched across broken glass - everywhere broken glass, flying through the air as though with kinetic energy - gingerly negotiating around debris that ranged from shop merchandise to human body parts, from display item shoes to shoes with feet still in them, and everything either crudely blackened, blood-soaked, or both.

I saw grown men - burly military types, army reservists, no doubt - break down in barely suppressed grief. Sirens wailed deafeningly, people even more so, as the awful extent of this mayhem began to hit home. Within minutes the whole area was sealed off, me in the middle surrounded by police, militia, photographers, reporters, TV camera crews, Hassidim...and bodies.

There was a sickly stench of death. I've not witnessed death before, other than in the movies, but the pungent wreak was unmistakable, the charred remains of objects inanimate and once animate littering the street like a crude piece of conceptual art. Body bags - I saw two, perhaps there were more - were loaded into Magen David Adom ambulances. This is not an easy thing to watch. Conversely, it is quite impossible *not* to watch, and as I did so it dawned on me what a horribly routine sight this must be in the Jewish homeland. And that I, who does not even live there, was not devastated by what I was witnessing was in itself quite devastating. The shock, delayed or otherwise, would doubtless come later.

I stood photographing the eerie sight of boots and shoes and tailors dummies being swept into black bags, as though in tasteless parody of the real human

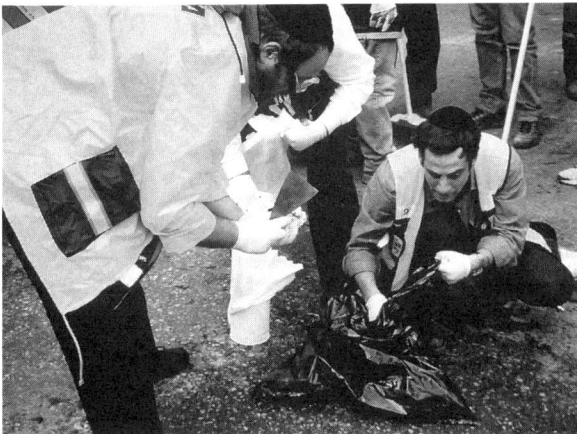

remains that were being scraped by Hassidim, with chisel and blade, up off the sidewalk and into what looked for all the world like supermarket 'snappy' bags. You cannot imagine what it is like to watch such a scene. It's not the horror that hit me, but the sheer casualness with which I found myself observing, photographing and recording the whole thing.

## TROUBLE IN PARADISE

I spoke to the guy closest to me, my sort of age, leather jacket, T-shirt, it could have been me. "What brings you here?" I asked, for he had no note-book, no camera, no seemingly official reason whatever to be within this tightly restricted cauldron. He gave me his card. Daniel Seamen. Director of Public Relations. Office of the Prime Minister. "And you?" he asked. "Usually a journalist, this week a tourist", I replied. "Visiting friends and photographing street scenes". These weren't the scenes I'd planned.

As I left the area, a score and more thoughts and emotions chasing through my head, the one clear view I had was that of the world's media shrouding their surface sympathy for Israel's dead and wounded in a tidal wave of they-only-bring-it-upon-themselves rhetoric. And if Israel must retaliate, they say, let them do so with their hands tied behind their back.

You had to be there to realise just how vulnerable this tiny little country is, a country where, if we're perfectly honest, it's not settlements and holy sites that are the issue, but Israel's very right to exist. The stoicism with which devastation is acknowledged and, to whatever extent, accepted on a daily basis is as depressing as it is palpable. You had to be there to hear shopkeeper and commuter, soldier and civilian, say: "This is how it is; life goes on".  But who ever said the line between stoicism and denial is anything other than very, very blurred, especially in Israel.

But then you walk down Jaffa Road, or Me'a Sha'arim, or wherever the latest bomb happened to explode, just a few short hours after the blast, you see the devastation somehow spirited away as though it never happened, a strange, somehow unsettling calm settling over the killing fields of just before, and you realise that this is, this really, *really* is, just another day in the life of a fledgling country whose pioneering dreams of an Eden-like existence lies in tatters.

For Jews there is no Eden, no seventy virgins at the gates of Paradise at the end of a suicide bombing. Inviting death, and then embracing it like a national flag, is not the Jewish way. Self-immolation and martyrdom simply do not have a place in the Jewish ethos. No cause is deemed worthy of dying for, and the idea of actually celebrating death - of oneself and of others - in the way some Palestinians appear to, to say nothing of accepting Sadaam's money in some sort of cash-for-suicide deal, is simply anathema to the Jewish people.

Life to us - to most people with rational train of thought - is more precious than that (not for nothing do Israeli forces invariably 'go in' at ground level, thereby minimising, wherever possible, civilian casualties, even at risk to their own), and as I sat on the sidewalk looking at a hand attached to nothing but tarmac, the realisation of how little regard some people have for human life - their own and others - just broke my heart.

And if any of this should sound a touch personal - and truly I'm trying so hard not to take sides - then I'm sorry. But it *is* personal. I have friends and family under constant fire, to say nothing of being hit upon myself, and try as I may to take a balanced view of matters, I do take attacks like this very, *very* personally.

When the dust died down - in all senses - and with those last thousand or so words hand-written from an improvised seat on a Jaffa Road kerb-side, I wended my way back up King George Street to Raymond's shop to tell him I was OK. He, it turns out, had been scouring the streets since the explosion, which he heard from the shop a hundred or so metres away, trying to find me. He'd even phoned home to ask Susan for my mobile number; not that he'd have reached me, not with the sirens, the wailing, the unholy commotion that would have drowned out the howling of a thousand and one mobile phones these past hours.

Anyway, having checked in with Raymond, phoned home, and phoned Allan (who, it occurred to me, might also have been trying to reach me, and, in fact, was), I returned to Hillel for an extremely late lunch before heading out to Gilo to visit Leonid and Mira, the very dearest of my ex-Soviet refusenik friends and, in Leonid, one of my most constant e-mail companions since modern technology and I first (and belatedly) became acquainted.

What a lovely evening we had, a whacking great dollop of fettuccini going down a treat at Kaffit, one of my favourite old eateries down on Emek Refa'im, right along the way from Nada bakery, they of the multi-flavoured challas that I used to buy each and every Erev Shabbat.

Back at Leonid and Mira's apartment - an apartment with a near-daily view of rolling tanks and freshly wasted mortar shells - my hosts reassured me as to their resolve to stay firm in the country to which they had fought so long and hard to emigrate. I sat and listened, at the same time typing up my notes and e-mailing my reflections of the day's events to various folk back home, before sharing a late night drink with my friends. And back at Mevasseret I slept the sleep I rather felt I'd earned.

This had been a very long day.

## DAY FOUR...

I met Leonid for coffee at his office, and was so impressed to see how incredibly well he's done as one of the top two or three electrical engineers in all of Jerusalem. He has a beautiful office in a compound that sits in rolling acres of manicured grounds, complete with multiple sports and leisure facilities. It is possible, just possible, that amenities of this kind were not on offer back in Leningrad, (and certainly not to someone who had committed the heinous crime of seeking to emigrate)...but I could be wrong.

From Leonid's office on, or pretty damn near, Sakharov Gardens I made for Hillel, where coffee and Danish beckoned, as did the photographic city tour I'd promised myself yesterday, before other events intervened and laid my plans to temporary waste.

## TROUBLE IN PARADISE

One small problem. The weather turned. And when I say turned, I mean really turned, in that horribly windy-rainy-squally way that Jerusalem seems to do quite remarkably well, on this occasion capturing quite perfectly the mood of the previous days debacle. What to do?

I answered my own question in a blinding flash. I drove back to Mevasseret, gathered up my gear, and headed down to the Dead Sea for a couple of days rest and relaxation at the Hyatt Regency Spa Resort.

The roads were empty, the sun shone brighter the further away I headed from Jerusalem, and the drive was altogether wonderful. It seems so long since I last drove south in Israel, and that first view of the Dead Sea's translucent turquoise waters, juxtaposed with the reds and yellows of the sea-shore, still takes the breath away, as it always did. If only there had been something for company other than Kuwaiti radio, which for some reason seems always to play louder and clearer within Israel's borders than Kol Yisroel. Mind you, they did manage to segue from "Virginia Plain" to "Watching the Detectives" as I approached Ein Gedi, so I'm disposed to set aside all ideological differences in the interests of top notch rock-and-roll.

Well, the Dead Sea resort area has certainly changed since I was last there. It used to be two hotels, one tumbledown hostel, and a solitary flea-ridden café attached to a - the - filling station. Now it's become a burgeoning oasis (if that's not a little oxymoronic), like Las Vegas with salt. There must be a score and more large hotels, spa resorts, and palaces of fun and pampering...and the Hyatt Regency is clearly the pick of the bunch, a stunningly landscaped triumph of hedonism and unfeasible vastness nestling in the considerable shadow of some hulking great flat topped mountains.

I made straight for the hotel's spa. First gym, then swim, and finally an hour long massage, which I can only assume was soothing and stress relieving, since I managed to sleep my way through pretty

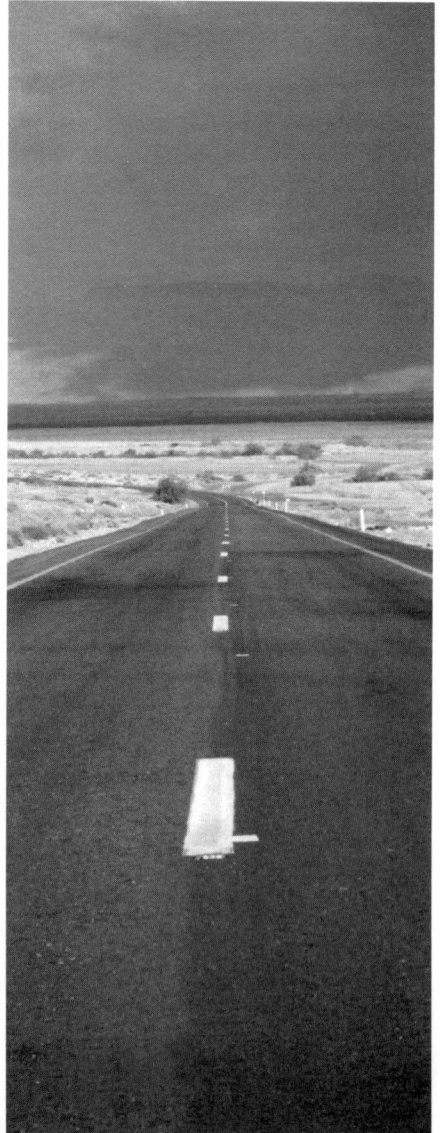

much the whole thing. My, but don't these new-age therapies sound exotic? When I asked for a detox herbal linen-wrap with glycolic acid and sea salt, I really wasn't at all sure whether I was ordering a massage or lunch.

It was great. I booked myself another, one through which I might stay awake. It was administered by a girl called Nurit, who proceeded to assault me with willow branches, lengths of twine, wet towels and buckets of icy cold water. And this in the country to which we Jews are supposed to have *escaped* from bondage.

All that remained was to have a facial. And all it takes, let me tell you, to ring my bells these days is to have my blackheads squeezed, plucked and discarded in a steamy hot booth by a sultry army reservist called Dalia. Bliss, sheer bliss, and never mind the myopic old bloke who kept coming in to my booth asking for the toilet, before cursing Dalia for cursing him, *and* criticizing her for the way she was wielding the tweezers.

"Don't be so rude", I said to him. "She's a lady".
"Why shouldn't I be rude?" he replied. "I'm Israeli".

Such disarming logic you can't argue with. Instead I lolled around the spa the rest of the day, before turning in for a ridiculously early night, accompanied by room service, CNN, and more room service. Those massages really knock you out.

## DAY FIVE...

Breakfast. Overload. Gluttony. Israeli breakfasts hold no truck with the concept of understatement, and in a manner that you'd have thought might have required some sort of planning consent, I piled my plate so high you could put a passenger lift up the middle and call it an office block. I ate myself silly; a dozen and one varieties of herring, enough eggy things to worry my cholesterol levels to death, and a bowl of Coco Pops.

An hour or so in the gym saw me right, by which time the sun had poked through just enough to beckon me to the shore of the Dead Sea's salty waters. I grabbed myself a recliner. I didn't really need to grab; there wasn't exactly a queue. The bathers, in fact, extended to me, a lady in a costume that seemed to be made almost entirely from cling-film, and a lifeguard, which in Israel means someone who did slightly better at swimming lessons than his school-mates, and knows how to demonstrate the hand signal that apparently means: "Oh shit, I'm drowning!"

The sun shone bright for fully half-an-hour, just enough to justify having crossed the road, before blue turned to grey and dry became not-so-dry. The heavens opened, pretty rare in these parts, but consistent with the prevailing dark mood of the country. No matter. I'd booked yet another facial and an Indian head massage, so I was happy enough to head on back to the spa and offer my pores to a girl called Ronit.

## TROUBLE IN PARADISE

That done - and very nice it was too - I took a leisurely lunch, before packing my kit bag and hitting the road back to the city, stopping heaven knows how often to photograph the astonishing and constantly changing colours of sea and mountains alike. The stretch of road that hugs the Dead Sea really is something else; vibrant, thrilling, and a million light years from the mayhem and civil unrest it leads to.

Back at Mevasseret, Raymond and I ordered a TV dinner and had a boys night in watching soccer, basketball and a couple of old movies.

ℭℨ

## DAY SIX...

This is the day I meant to have on Sunday - walking around Jerusalem taking *nice* photos, not blown up shops, blown out windows, and random body parts. The sun came out, the mercury rose, and I could hardly wait to get out there, so much so I was up at 7 and breakfasting at Hillel before 8.

Well, thank God the sun did shine. It was the one and only barrier to the kind of depression brought on by watching such an aesthetically beautiful city starve itself of tourists, money and life. The place was empty, the dearth of people at the Western Wall such that virtually the entire stretch of wall was visible to the naked eye.

I don't much care for the Kotel. It's segregated, it's exclusivist, and it has, even in its relative emptiness, a dark air of brooding fundamentalism hanging over every brick, every stone, every Hassid, and every sentry guard. And with each person that tries to scam money off you for one or other bogus charity, it is religious commercialism *in extremis*, and about as spiritual as a dog kennel.

That said, the Dome of the Rock glittered and glistened with a heavenly radiance, and under brilliant blue skies you could almost believe this was a good place to be. But then I was subjected to my umpteenth panhandling of the day, and reality bit once more.

I parked myself in one of the Old City's gorgeously reconstituted old squares - I think it was Ha'mekubalim Street - cappuccino in my hand, yeshiva kids at my feet, soldiers all around, and it was mightily hard to shift the notion that the planners, had they been trying to come up with a hybrid of Crown Heights, Anatevka and Edgware, succeeded with flying colours - except, perhaps, the soldiers.

The kids - urchins with bagels I call them - are everywhere, running wild, *payot* flying around their faces like personal stereo headphones, and not an adult in sight to rein them in; which is fair enough, for, odd though it may seem in this of all cities, this little square has an aura of near impenetrable peace and tranquillity. Truly you'd never know the evils and horrors that lie just around the corner, strapped to the waist of a Paradise-seeking terrorist.

After meandering through the Old City's Cardo shopping mall - empty, absolutely empty, not a soul in sight - I made for the gym at the David Citadel, and then to Allan and Roberta's for a night's board and lodging and a few home comforts, which in my case need extend no further than toasted challa and Marmite and a hot Ribena.

ভ

## DAY SEVEN...

Up and out before 7, it was so good to catch the sun playing over the Old City from the Tayelet, the lovely promenade right around from our old flat in Armon Hanatziv. God knows how much film I got through, and God knows how much nostalgia seeped into my system, as I gazed across the valley at dawn's peaceful breaking across the few square miles that still manage to steal my affections from under my nose.

I drove to the Sheraton, parked up courtesy of the protexia Roberta - as a senior Sheraton staffer - brings to these situations, and strolled through the park, under what by now was a quite radiant burst of sunshine, to my breakfast table at Hillel. I hurried coffee and croissant in double quick time to catch the best of the brilliant blue skies, and wandered down Ben Yehuda to sit a while in Kikar Zion.

## TROUBLE IN PARADISE

I was just marvelling at the blissful peace that seemed to reign - frankly if a bomb isn't going off somewhere around you in Jerusalem these days, that constitutes blissful peace - when a bomb went off. Or at least it sounded like a bomb. Certainly it was the mother, the grandmother, the great-great-great-grandmother of big bangs. Sirens kicked in without a beat; the deafening wall of sound that seems as commonplace as whatever trauma and catastrophe it accompanies in this crazy, troubled, sad town.

Pandemonium was about to let rip once more on the city centre. Deja vu was about to set in. About to, but not quite. For just as suddenly as the noise erupted, the noise abated. I don't know why, and I wasn't about to stick around to find out. One bomb a week, that's about my limit. And anyway, I had just a few brief hours left in town and I wanted to get back to my sunny little square in the Old City.

I was there before 9.30. It was empty, save for me and the odd backpacker or two...and a lone accordion player who was content to bang out *Yerushelayim Shel Zahav,* Jerusalem The Golden, without the barest hint of irony. Jerusalem may be golden in appearance...but in spirit? I'm not so sure.

Whatever. I sat an hour or two, soaking up the sun - and the odd cappuccino - while the flow of pedestrian traffic increased somewhat; mostly locals, precious few tourists, and all stopping a moment or two to bask in the relative serenity en route to their yeshiva, their sentry post, their pathetically vulnerable city centre shoe shop or pizza parlour, or wherever. The morning passed pleasantly, quietly, peacefully, and reflectively...and then it was time to go.

And as I took my seat on the plane back to London, I knew that before long I'd be logging on to my e-mails, my heart sinking to see the name either of Judith, Leonid, or Allan at the top of the screen, and wondering - like waiting for that late night phone call on news of an ailing relative - what terrible tidings their message would bring the morning after the atrocity before.

Judith said to me last e-mail: "We have a pretty good life; a beautiful country, wonderful family values, *never a dull moment* ". After seeing what I saw at first hand on the streets of Jerusalem, I rather wish life for Judith, and all my other friends in Israel, would, in the nicest possible way, be dull.

Frankly, I'm not optimistic. But as Golda Meier said: "Pessimism is a luxury no Jew can allow himself". Perhaps she's right.

‍ಞ

# LOYD GROSSMAN KNEW MY FATHER

My horse wore an expression that suggested it
was dependant on a diet of Prozac and Rioja to
see it through the day. His name was Speedy.
He wasn't. In a head to head race between
Speedy and Professor Stephen Hawking, I'd
back the guy in the chair.

## Eight great journeys

It was like a scene from a Laurel and Hardy film, the one where Stan and Ollie have only to open a car door for the whole damn thing to collapse in an irredeemable heap of twisted metal and crankshafts. That's how it was for me in Cuba each time I fell off, overturned, capsized or just plain destroyed one or other vehicle at my disposal.

My mission was to cross Cuba in tandem with my daughter Lucy by as many modes of transport as possible, a daft concept that sat up begging for air the minute we stepped out of the iconoclastic Hotel Nacional and hit the streets of Havana. The Nacional is a gem. Palm trees to the front, regimental cannons to the rear, and on the inside that eerily deserted feeling, oddly reminiscent of the hotel in *The Shining*, that has you waiting on the edge of your seat for an eyeball popping Jack Nicholson to bust through the door wielding a sawn-off machete.

With twin towers that must surely one day be removed, transported, and placed atop the new Wembley Stadium, and a lobby as long as the stadium itself, the hotel is as expansive as those said to have whiled away the odd daiquiri or two on its oceanfront lawns - Marlon Brando and Winston Churchill come to mind - though frankly the surrounding area, the Vedado, is so grimly grey and unprepossessing it was hard to escape the notion, once outside the hotel, that I'd dozed off on the plane and slept through the entire hijacking, awaking only once we'd been diverted to Neasden.

For all of its acclaimed complexity and contrast - vibrancy and dereliction, bustling bars and empty shops, Communism and the Caribbean, in essence pre-Glasnost-Moscow-with-better-music - Havana's big thing is transport, bizarre transport, and not just the bulbous old Chevvys and Buicks that seem to recall Elvis and the words *Girls, Girls, Girls.*

If the cars evoke another era - and frankly the whole of Havana does - then the public transport suggests much input from the surrealist school of automotive engineering. From the ubiquitous Coco taxi - a hollowed-out yellowy-orange metallic satsuma on wheels from which someone has quite literally taken the pith - to the decidedly odd-looking Camel - a low-slung lorry-drawn tram, the middle of whose three carriages looks like Orson Welles was dropped onto it from a very great height - the whole thing looks like a scene from *Wacky Races*.

## LOYD GROSSMAN KNEW MY FATHER

Lucy and I sampled all these conveyances and more. But it was the Hemingway ride we were after, across Cuba by horseback. I'm no Hemingway fan myself. To me Fat Ernest was jut a boozed-up old fart with a sleazy line in whoring and an unspeakable line in vulgarity, a man who is said to have broken wind with such ferocity whilst riding his steed across the Cordillera de Guaniguanico, he ruptured two discs at the base of his spine while severely impairing the hearing of both himself and his horse. But he certainly knew his bum from his bridle and I, for one, was happy enough to follow in his hoof-prints.

I met my horse as I stepped from my rudderless and fast submerging speedboat - don't ask how, it just sort of happened - after a hair-brained race with a fleet of Colombian skinheads down the blissfully tranquil Rio Canimar. I say blissful. Obviously it once *was* blissful, but on this very day it resembled, quite uncannily, the Poll Tax Riots on water.

The meeting point for rider and horse was a loose affiliation of distempered straw huts masquerading as a stud farm on the banks of the river. My hopes weren't high. Just as well, really. The old nag wore an expression that suggested it was dependant on a diet of Prozac and Rioja to see it through the day. If I didn't know better I'd say it had been crying. But worse - and this was very bad news indeed - it stood barely thirteen hands in its stockinged feet. In equine terms this rendered it eligible to be ridden by a 3-year old. It was only the absence of starter wheels and a little silver key that convinced me it was the real thing and not some wind-up number from Toys R Us.

This vole with a saddle was called Speedy, a gentle slice of Caribbean irony or a flagrant contravention of the Trades Description Act, depending on your point of view. As donkeys go I've see Tony Adams move faster. I mean no ill will to either party when I say this, but in a head to head race between Speedy and Professor Stephen Hawking, I'd back the guy in the chair.

Lucy's horse was smaller still, measurable in digits rather than cubits. In twelve short years my daughter went from reading My Little Pony to riding it. No matter. Our steeds had eight legs between them and that was all we needed to set forth for a day in the saddle.

Together we rode a path that hugged with great intimacy the water's edge. Vultures soared overhead, eagles even higher, while the resplendent tocororo bird, with its red, white and blue of the Cuban flag, swooped alongside us and guided our way. The vista was heavenly and on faster horses we might have made it all the way south to the Zapata Peninsula.

We did attain higher speeds 48 hours later. In fact we got up to around 40 miles an hour before it all went horribly wrong. I made to turn right, my mount went left, and we all went sprawling along a dirt track road. My legs were cut to tatters, my ego to ribbons. This is what happens when you trade your horse for a motor-bike - ancient Harley Davidson to be precise, the kind Steve McQueen used to ride over fences with the Luftwaffe in hot pursuit, the type I was now riding with Lucy in hot pursuit, glued to my back like a Siamese twin, and thus able to walk away from the whole mangled mess perfectly unscathed as I careened along the gravel on my front with Lucy still attached to my rear, holding on for dear life. These are the kind of things you don't tell your insurance company.

We biked in Varaderro, the Costa del Cuba and a haven for Germanic towel throwing of the highest order. Lucy and I were up for a bit of speed - horses, Harleys, anything to escape the Nuremberg Towels. The trouble is Varaderro is a one horse town, and the town's one horse had already been hired out. "No problem", Mr. One-Horse-For-Hire said. "You take my bike; she go faster than Mr. Sheen". It took me a week to figure out he meant Barry, not the furniture polish.

The rest is history, but to finish the story Lucy laughed long, loud and theatrically at my staggering incompetence, before bending to the road and handing me something irreparably broken and distinctly engine-like. It was the engine, and it was broken, very broken indeed. The walk back to the hotel was long and painful, the more so for Lucy whose sides were by now seriously aching from all that hilarity. "It wasn't my fault", I said to Mr. One-Horse-For-Hire, as I stood, slightly sheepishly, dribbling screws, bolts and assorted engine parts from every pocket. I thought he was going to cry. Was he related to the horse, I wondered?

**JEEP SAFARI** the poster in the hotel lobby said. "You're a good driver" Lucy said. "What could possibly go wrong?" There we were the next day, twenty of us in a ten

jeep convoy, doing anything and everything to break out of Varaderro and free ourselves from the sausage-sucking, bicep-flexing, belly-flopping human pyramids that had colonised this

# LOYD GROSSMAN KNEW MY FATHER

Teutonic corner of Cuba. It was like *Escape From Colditz*, a bunch of incarcerated Englishmen in Bermuda shorts and Reebok trainers tunnelling out of the compound with teaspoons and driving licences.

And while we're on the subject, just what is it about Germans that makes them so insufferably objectionable on holiday? I don't mean to generalise, and truly I have the utmost respect for the current generation of Germans. They have - and this much is on the record and beyond all manner of dispute - moved mountains to make amends for the Germany of a half-century ago, and they are in all senses to be commended and congratulated for their enlightenment, endeavour and, for the most part, cultural and ethnic tolerance. Indeed, such has been the radical shift in socio-political emphasis in modern day Germany that the German Jewish community now flourishes like no other in Western Europe, attracting Jewish émigrés in their thousands from the former Soviet Union and even from Israel. Yes; Germany has come a long way in a short time, and fair play to them for that.

And yet...put a German in a swimsuit, a fluffy towelling robe and a pair of plastic flip-flops and he becomes the holiday camp commandant of your darkest dreams, annexing large swathes of swimming pool and commandeering deck-chairs by the lorry-load. And worse, they're so damn competitive, their desire to win exceeded only by their pathological need to arrive everywhere ahead of everyone else. God, I'd love to have seen them on the Titanic, just as the sirens went off, throwing their towels over the life belts.

And they're so gung-ho, and so unfeasibly jolly - this is a nation, remember, without any known tradition of humour - concocting and then organising games from activities that are so brainless they would surely have been jettisoned even by the BBC's late and surely never-to-be-lamented Friday night feast of fun, "It's a Knockout". One of these games at our Varaderro hotel entailed running around the perimeter of the pool with a bottle of wine between your legs while holding a melted ice-cream cone in one hand, a floppy penis-like object in the other - Germans do love a floppy penis-like object - and performing some sort of elaborate mime to Wagner's "Ride of the Valkyries". Another involved ice-cube spitting and tea-bag throwing for which, frankly, there is no explanation.

I simply do not have words adequate to commentate coherently on such wilful inanity, such alarming silliness. Suffice to say the prize for the winner was a bowl of soup, a commodity Germans seem to value even more highly than floppy penis-like objects. I have no idea why this should be. I was well out of my depth by now, seriously confused, and yes, even a little troubled by what I was witnessing. Heaven alone knows what Stuart Hall and dear old Eddie Waring would have made of it all.

Needless to say the Germans won every last competition. God knows how they lost two wars. Had they had beach balls and custard pies instead of mortar shells and doppelgangers I'm sure we'd all be part of Greater Germany by now.

One of the Germans - a very nice guy called Werner - spotted my Star of David neck-chain and asked me where my family originated. "My father's side were Russian", I said. "Please to tell me", he replied, his shoulders heaving in that

Edward-Heath-just-heard-a-joke kind of a way, "that your father was not linesman in 1966 World Cup Final". Laugh? I nearly dropped my liverwurst.

I was very taken with Werner, in particular his very strange accent which, perhaps on account of his having lived a while in upstate Massachusetts, made him sound uncannily like the bastard love-child of Marlene Dietrich and Loyd Grossman. I invited him to join Lucy and me out on the open road, but he graciously declined, preferring instead to concoct some or other new fountain of hilarity involving a pelican, a cucumber and a push-up brassiere.

Still, back to the jeep safari. We were assigned our vehicles and proceeded to blaze a rubbery trail up hills, down dales and over bridges and dried out river beds, bumping and grinding our way in and out of crater-sized potholes, along off-road tracks that were so off road they weren't even tracks. Through the bowels of the Matanzas province we charted territory hitherto uncharted by the humble Suzuki Jeep.

All went well until you-know-who decided to make a break for it and shot off down the autopista towards the cigar-making town of Pinar del Rio. I raced through the gears, both of them, and spun the rev counter all the way round and into the red bit. Now this was fast. How fast I didn't realise until I felt a sudden and heroically cold blast of wind that had no right or reason to be there with the roof closed. I looked up. Above me, sky. My roof had blown clean off, a stunning debacle even by my standards. "It wasn't my fault", I pleaded to Mr. Ten-Jeeps-For-Hire back at Varaderro. The penny dropped. "Aah", he said, "you're the guy with the bike".

The safer haven of the saddle beckoned once more, an extensive search of the peninsula eventually yielding a pair of high velocity horses to gallop along the golden sands under brilliant blue skies and a gorgeously warming sun. It was glorious, man and beast in perfect union on a soft surface utterly conducive to high speeds and an uncommonly comfy ride. And when we were done with equine transport we hitched ourselves a couple of jet skis and skimmed across the surf to the little tropical islands on the horizon with only the most minor of mishaps, though the dolphin that finds my wallet might care to note that neither of my credit cards have much credit left on them.

But for all our derring-do on the high sierra and the high seas, it was on the music-filled streets and plazas of Old Havana that we found the essential Cuba. The sound of Havana is the Buena Vista Social Club, the troupe of ancient Cuban minstrels unearthed, re-assembled, and strategically placed in tuxedos and concert halls a few years back by the legendary slide guitar player and occasional Rolling Stones sideman Ry Cooder.

In truth Buena Vista aren't especially good. Their singing is quivery rather than strident, their playing competent rather than virtuoso, and you're left admiring, perhaps even sharing, the obvious joy they bring one another just by being alive and playing, yet wishing somehow that they'd cut loose just once in a while, rip it up and belt out something like "Anarchy in the UK", while at the same time smashing their guitars against the nearest amplifier. But they *are* old and that gives them, I guess, a certain gravitas, and if they want to give it some large to audiences hung up on the word 'authentic' before hanging up their mandolins and joining the celestial choir above, then who am I to deny them this final gig or two.

Their music is played on the streets of Havana by pretty much anyone with a stringed instrument and a cloth cap. It fills every crack and every corner of the city, a wizened old guitar picker in every doorway, and if you hear the tune "Chan Chan" less than twenty times in any one Havana day…well… you're probably not in Havana. Either that or you're extremely deaf.

Chevvys and Chan Chan apart, the image that lingers longest since returning from Cuba is the view from the Nacional over the Malecon, the Havana sea-front promenade that stretches from the mouth of the Almendares River all the way along the front to the fortress-like Castillo de la Punta at the northern end of the Prado, Old Havana's tree-lined and architecturally beguiling main thoroughfare.

The Prado is the hub of everything in Havana, an avenue given to much posturing and people-watching, like Barcelona's Ramblas without the flower sellers, or Rome's Via Condotti without the million dollar stores, but with a handful of mansions and former presidential palaces that are as appealing on the outside as they are decrepit within. Such is the way in Havana. If you've been to St. Petersburg you'll know what I mean.

The Malecon's erosion-battered buildings are a sight to behold, cruelly scarred by the mighty waves that hit the sea wall before bouncing up and over and onto the streets, drenching anyone and anything that gets in their way. You can time the waves, especially the big thirty footers, like contractions, but you can never escape them. Walk within a hundred yards and they'll get you every time, which renders all the more capricious the kids who play on the rocks, the old men who come to fish, and the bright young things who gather at sunset for a chinwag and a jar or two of rum perched up on the sea wall.

Ultimately, though, the car is the thing in Cuba, and at last, on our final day, we got to hitch a ride in the back of a seriously antiquated and utterly fabulous Firebird, the one with a grille the height of an office block and a foldaway "dicky" seat that pops out of the boot at the grinding of an antediluvian lever. Oh how we preened, oh how we posed, as we cruised past the Bodeguita del Medio, the Hemmingway wannabes putting down their mojitos for a glimpse of this ridiculous old Jew and his pretty blonde daughter. "Once more round the block", I said to our driver, as we completed our fifteenth lap of the Plaza de Armas, luxuriating in the mottled leather of the car's open rear end for all of Havana to see.

And then - don't ask me why - I was fiddling with the up-down mechanism of the dicky when my watch got caught on something sharp down the back of the seat, slipped off my wrist onto something called a wheel-bearing, causing the single most stomach wrenching noise you ever heard, a fingernails-scratching-down-the-blackboard-meets-crunching-on-broken-glass kind of sound, and the upshot is the car doesn't go any more. "Stanley…there's another fine mess….."

# PLACES BEGINNING WITH 'B'

Lake Titicaca + La Paz + the Salt Lakes of
Uyuni + the suicidally madcap Yungas Road +
priests who baptise Japanese motor cars + a
girl called Rivka and her environment-friendly
orgasms = my favourite country of all.  My roots
are in England, but my heart is in Bolivia.

## Eight great journeys

I've always liked places beginning with B. I grew up on the beaches of Brighton and Bournemouth (my daughter now resides in the former, my son the latter, at their respective universities), stayed with my granddad in Bayswater and an aunt in Broxbourne, and my favourite European cities are Bergen, Budapest and Salamanca, which technically doesn't begin with 'B', but you'll allow me that one, I hope. Belgium rather lets the side down, but then Europe has never been strong on countries beginning with B.

Perhaps that's what drew me to Bolivia.

&#8478;

## CARELESS, SO CARELESS...

Dropping out of the sky into La Paz, I felt like a cornflake drifting lazily down into some kind of gigantic cereal bowl.

OK, strange analogy. But how else to convey the image of a plane-load of mortals descending from a very great height into what I can only describe as an immense amphitheatre, which, to all intents and purposes, is what La Paz is. A sunken city, two-and-a-half miles in the sky, yet utterly cocooned by a perfectly circular wall of mountains, some of them a further two miles higher, to which a cluster of shanty villages seem valiantly determined to cling for fear of sliding down the hill and losing their very fine vantage point.

That first view of La Paz was everything I hoped it would be, everything I expected it to be, everything I was told it would be, and it didn't disappoint. A sight once seen, never forgotten, particularly as I had not expected to see it quite so soon.

Let me explain.

I'm careless, perhaps the most careless man ever to walk the face of the Earth. I'm careless with crockery, careless with house keys, careless with personal stereo systems, and I'm frighteningly careless with double yellow lines, which - and for someone with a finely tuned sense of colour this is particularly worrying - I rarely seem to notice when parking my car on the streets of London, thereby accruing a body of financial penalties that could bring down a small Central European republic. But most of all I'm careless, almost terminally so, when it comes to assimilating the simplest, most basic written information, even when it's printed in block capitals the size of Bolton.

The fact is, you see, I wasn't meant to be in Bolivia at all, not at the start of my Latin American Y2002 odyssey. My itinerary, adaptable though it turned out to be, clearly provided for Brazil first, Bolivia last, and a large sweep of Western Hemisphere in between, to include meeting up with my wife in Belize, my daughter in Cuba, and my son in Florida (which is not at all Latin, but I'd sooner not play my tennis on dusty old South American clay courts, thank you very much, not with Versace tennis tops at 125 bucks a throw).

My time-table was sacrosanct. I had it in writing, from my tour operator, my newspaper, and my friend Freddie in Costa Rica, who had just three days in the whole fiscal quarter when he was free to spend time with me. And my time in Ecuador was even more specifically time-tied, as I was to help one of their adventure travel companies plot and plan new treks for new trekkers, along with a mountain guide pal of mine from New Southgate who I was to meet up with at a specified time and place in Quito.

And now my plans - God, it would be hilarious if it weren't so stupid - were blown to Botswana and back in the blinking of an apparently myopic eye.

What can I tell you? I got on the wrong bloody plane at Heathrow bloody airport, an act of fecklessness on my part matched only by that of the ground staff who let me onto a La Paz-bound plane with a Rio-bound ticket in the first place, thereby casting into serious doubt the future placing of the words 'airport' and 'security' in the same sentence.

Still, no harm done. In fact, much good done. A glaring error by the airline (note how I've now *totally* shifted responsibility in this matter; an unashamedly male trait, it must be said), a shameless and somewhat theatrical thrusting of my press card in the face of a seriously stressed stewardess, and a first class upgrade was mine for the taking, all I required to spare the wonderful folk of KLM from the sharper end of my ballpoint. Isn't it marvellous? Just three square inches of plastic is all it took to secure me de luxe carriage, gourmet dining and that fabulous, mysterious curtain that separates the riff-raff from the hoi polloi, albeit on the wrong plane to the wrong country.

☙

That heavenly first view of La Paz etched into my soul, I made straight for the hotel who were to have been my hosts some…well…several weeks later. As luck would have it they had room for me, plenty of it, which is either a good sign or a bad sign, depending on your degree of optimism.

I'm a pessimist by nature, but so chuffed was I by this huge slice of good fortune after my stunning geographical debacle, and so impressed was I with my capacity to continually surprise myself with my own daftness - there are those, I believe, who would find it all rather endearing - I just dumped my stuff in an unceremonious heap in Room 207 of the Hotel El Rey Palace before scurrying downstairs and making for the streets of La Paz. I pulled up sharp in the hotel lobby. There was a guy sitting on the sofa surrounded by an ocean of maps and guidebooks, and all of them written suspiciously from right to left.

"Shalom. Ma Shlom'cha", I said to the man with the Hebrew literature. Actually my Hebrew is rather better than just "Hi, how's it going", but speak to an Israeli in passable Hebrew and the odds are he'll come back at you with perfect English, *and* with a better accent. Game, set and match, the English language, and never mind all those Hebrew words I know, but somehow never get to use.

Running into Israelis in La Paz is not so unusual as you might think, given that half of Israel seems to be trekking and traipsing around South America these days, particularly post-army kids intent on discovering post-army life as far from home as possible, smoking dope with the Dalai Lama up in the Himalayas and chomping on roasted llama down in Guayaquil.

The guy with the Hebrew literature was a little older, and together with his pal had arrived just recently from Tel Aviv to lend weight to the local Israeli embassy, one as temporary ambassador, the other to help initiate some sort of drugs awareness programme - which is kind of strange, because I'd always thought Bolivians knew all there was to know about drugs.

Ami and Eyal, those were their names, and as veterans of 48 hours in La Paz - two days, and already they had a day off? - they offered to walk me the length and breadth of the downtown district and show me the sights. I accepted the offer and together we walked and talked, Eyal filling my head with facts, figures and a veritable encyclopaedia of drug-related information.

"Did you know", he asked, "that as recently as ten years ago the livelihoods of more than 40% of Bolivia's workforce was wholly dependent on the illicit production and trafficking of cocaine?"

As it happens I did know. We'd probably read the same guide book.

"And did you know", he continued, "that over 80% of all those caught trafficking are known to have organised crime ties?"

"The answer is simple", I replied. "If you don't want to get caught, don't wear the tie".

My little joke was lost on Eyal, as he steamrollered on with the lecture. Some of it was actually quite interesting, like the decision of the United States to get involved in the 90s by mounting some sort of coca crop eradication scheme. Even back then, pre-Bush Junior, they were geographically challenged, a certain up-and-coming congressman suggesting that they "spray the Bolivian coca crop with herbicides dropped by planes based on a carrier off the Bolivian coast". For those unacquainted with The Americas, this is tantamount to you or me trying to book a beach holiday in Switzerland.

And so it went, walking and talking, until our first port of call was reached. The Israeli quarter. Officially there is no Israeli quarter, or indeed Jewish quarter, in La Paz. With a resident Jewish population stopping well short of the thousand mark, why should there be? But with shop windows adorned in Spanish and Hebrew, and internet cafes peopled almost exclusively, it seemed, by husky young Sabras, I feel comfortable enough conferring upon this district the title of Little Israel.

As young Israelis munched on felafel and pitta bread and schmoozed the day away, all around us the streets throbbed and hummed to the beat of students and workers, as they marched and demonstrated the length of the city's principal thoroughfare, the Prado, in rumbustious, good natured anarchy.

Women in trilbys and bowlers ignored the whole thing as they sat on the sidewalk peddling their wares. Tiny children, stricken with terminal shoe-shine syndrome, hustled for every penny they could make, shining people's shoes with a breathtaking

indifference as to whether or not the recipient had actually asked for a shine. Even less relevant was whether or not the recipient was wearing open sandals, and in some cases they were. Actually you could walk barefoot in La Paz and still get a spit and polish.

And the more people spilled out onto the Prado, the more shoes became scuffed, and the more shoes became scuffed, the closer the kids came to morphing into a toddlers' empire called Shoe Shine Plc. Rampant commercialism is alive and well in La Paz and driving the freshly de-diapered out of a world of pooh-poohs and nappies and into the world of high finance.

The Prado is La Paz's answer to Barcelona's La Ramblas, a broad avenue with an almost permanently festive atmosphere. This is especially so on Sundays, when the lower Prado - this road divides itself into upper, middle and lower, and undergoes a half dozen or so name changes along the way - is closed to traffic, allowing the sidewalks to overflow with vendors of balloons and candy floss, and a multitude of revellers hiring kites, bikes, and dinky little dodgem cars (which aren't really dodgems, but that's how Bolivians drive). It's hard not to feel very, very alive on the Prado, and terribly easy to believe you've landed in the cradle of civilization.

My first afternoon in La Paz was an absolute joy, and I couldn't thank the embassy guys enough for the induction. And as the sun begun to drift slowly down to the horizon, the Israelis and I went our own sweet ways, they to the embassy office block - La Paz's largest, and heroically bedecked in the largest Israeli flag I ever saw outside of the Knesset - and me to the Café Ciudad, fabled 24-hour hangout where the big attraction - and it certainly isn't the food, not unless you like your linguini cold and your fruit juice warm - is the wall-to-wall televised sport that belts out, day and night, from the monster TV screen up on the wall.

From the Ciudad's vantage point on the Plaza del Estudiante all life is laid out before you, and many fine buildings too, virtually in a straight line along the length and breadth of the Prado. To one side, the handsome Libraria Don Busco and the stately Museo Archeologico de Tiwanaku; and to the other, the glitzy hotels that have not as yet - and I thank God for it - brought to La Paz any semblance of tourist overload.

And as I gazed out of the window, across the street and over this fascinating hybrid of modern and colonial buildings to the majestic volcanoes across the way, my altitude headache was forgotten, the airport cock-up - actually my cock-up, but why split hairs, especially when I've already shifted responsibility so shamelessly - was a thing of the past, and I felt as I always do on South American soil…wonderfully and quite inexplicably at home.

I strolled a leisurely stroll back to the hotel, hit the pillow for a quick pre-dinner snooze, and woke 14 hours later for breakfast.

☙

## FELAFEL AND PHALLUSES

Breakfast in the fifth floor dining room, overlooking pink churches, glass towers, and snow-capped mountains, was inspiring. Not the breakfast, you understand - though it was fine - but the views. As you peer down on the city - and so many are the opportunities for peering down from a great height in La Paz - you realise what a paradox this urban conurbation is. Vast yet compact, sprawling yet intimate, cosmopolitan yet parochial, colourful as a wacky kaleidoscope, and friendly like an eager puppy. The city vibrates with effortless ease to the rhythm of the people, as only a Latin city can. Pan pipes and percussion - gets me every time.

Ruben, my guide, picked me up at 8.30 for the city tour and the Moon Valley trek. Good start. We stalked the back streets, the Witches' Market, the fruit and veg market, the you-name-it-we've-got-it market, the plazas, the avenidas, the cathedrals, the Gold Museum, the Inca Museum - and my, don't the Incas like to display a gigantic great phallus or two, and never mind the emasculated feelings they engender in the average-hung Y-fronted tourist - and the seemingly never-ending array of fancy dress costumiers - scores of them - that leave you in no doubt as to how much partying, how many carnivals, and how much excess this town can get through.

We walked in the road for the most part, craving the indulgence of motorists whose expertise behind the wheel seems, as it does across most of South America, severely compromised by the brood of kids on their laps, and the very distinct possibility that the humble driving test is something that just happens to other people.

As to why we walked in the road...well...pavements are not for walking on in La Paz. They constitute valuable trading space. So many people selling knick-knacks and shoe-shines, alpaca and chewing gum, more gigantic great phalluses (the ones that didn't make it into the museum, I presume), and so, so many amulets, mostly of the llama foetus in resin variety, which are said to bring great good fortune to the purchaser, if not to the llama.

At every turn the views astound. Edinburgh, Florence, Hong Kong, San Fransisco; they're like the Fens compared to La Paz. And at every turn poverty and prosperity rub shoulders in curious juxtaposition, the scruffiest of street urchins scamming their pennies outside the chicest of cafes, cross-legged bowler-hatted ladies defying you not to trip over their merchandise as you step into your posh hotel.

We sheltered from the noonday sun in the shaded cloisters of the Cathedral of Our Mother of Peace on the Plaza Murillo, before crossing the square to the handsome, almost Havana-like Presidential Palace, bathed in a tranquility that belied the sheer weight of people milling around. That's the beauty of the big city. If it has enough heart you can find yourself enveloped by the masses and still feel gloriously lost in space.

Legs were traded for wheels as Ruben and I drove up to the little park at Mirador Killi Killi for the generally acknowledged best overview of the city. We gazed out to the peak of the mighty Mt. Illimani, all 22,000 feet of it, then down to the national soccer stadium, which stands in the heartland of downtown as something of a metaphor for the city itself, a vertiginous amphitheatre within a vertiginous amphitheatre. Playing at 12,000 feet must be like a suicide mission for most visiting teams. Small wonder Bolivia rarely lose a home game. You need more than a puff or two of Ventolin to play football two-and-a-half miles in the sky.

We continued our drive up to Moon Valley, a quite spectacularly beguiling confection of Grand Canyonesque red mountains and cactus groves. Reaching the valley itself entailed a downwards trek over such moon-like terrain - a surreal maze of pinnacles and canyons, craters and ravines - you wonder why Armstrong and Aldrin bothered shlepping all the way to the Moon when they had such an authentic lunarscape right on their doorstep. They'd have saved on petrol, they'd have got their photos developed way quicker, and they'd have come back with one hell of a shine on their moon boots.

This particular trek is most definitely not for the faint of heart. At every turn lies a deep and forbidding crevace to be negotiated...and for negotiated, read hurdled, sometimes with a run-up that suggested the beckoning of an all-American long jump medal. The setting is awesome - jagged, rugged, and worryingly unpredictable with sheer drops every which way you step; an idiot's playground if ever I saw one. I felt very at home.

We lunched - and boy, did we ever earn it - in a sheltered garden way down the hillside in the rather posh suburb of Miraflores. This gave me an early induction to the distinct possibility that in all of Bolivia's long and colourful history, not once have the words *cholesterol* and *problem* ever resided in the same sentence, paragraph or conversation.

Meat, meat, meat and meat, with a side order of anything fried, followed by cream, cream, ice cream, and cream...and all of it with whipped cream which, were such a thing possible, had first floated, alongside a tub of lard and a slab of suet, for the better part of a week in the bowels of a deep fat fryer. I didn't eat much.

Instead I asked Ruben if I might be dropped back at Restaurant El Lobo down on the corner of Illampu and Calle Santa Cruz. El Lobo is famous in these parts. It is Israeli-run, almost exclusively Israeli-frequented, with food, ambience and internet facility that are clearly geared to please the hordes, the hundreds upon hundreds of young Israeli post-army backpackers, that pass through Bolivia at almost any given time of the year. Ruben duly obliged, but not before consuming a potted cow or two in jelly.

I arrived at El Lobo with a rare thirst and proceeded to drink my way through a bewildering array of juices, shakes and colas, whilst trying my hand at a Spanish crossword in the local paper. Six drinks and approximately 85 pence later I hit the streets of La Paz refreshed and replenished, blithely caught up in what I now came to realise is the daily tea-time procession of underpaid, out-of-work, and generally put-upon workers and non-workers of this great city.

The streets were heaving, pavements piled high with people, and it was fully five minutes before I realised I was having my boots cleaned against my will. I peered down at a dewy-eyed ragamuffin who looked more world-weary than any self-respecting six-year-old should. With a hangdog expression that was one part Clement Freud, nine parts Deputy Dawg, he seemed for all the world as though the full weight of missed mortgage payments and multiple parking convictions were bearing down on his tiny shoulders. That said, he did a great job on my manky old boots, so fair play to young Mr. Shoe Shine. My boots sparkled like diamonds, the kid rooked me for double wages, and we both walked away happy.

Back at the hotel I phoned home, soaked in a hot tub, watched an Israeli guy knock Pete Sampras out of some Italian tennis tournament, and felt sufficiently rejuvenated to return to El Lobo for a falafel supper.

The joint was doing the proverbial jump. I never saw so many Israelis outside of West Hampstead. And given Israelis know how to eat, I can think of a lot worse jobs than owning this particular establishment. There must have been a hundred and more paying customers, and not one of them - myself excepted - above the age of twenty. It's only my natural vanity, coupled with my reckless refusal to act my age, that stopped me from feeling old. OK; that's bullshit. I felt old.

I noshed myself to a standstill before stepping back out onto the Calle Santa Cruz. From the brow of the hill it was possible to see, with a little help from the car lights, street lights, and flashing neon lights, almost all the five mile expanse of this gaping great crater of a city. The trees that lined the central promenade of the main thoroughfare were aglow with fairy lights, the leaves lit up like bottle-green Catherine wheels. Even after dark La Paz is a riot of colour. It was Guy Fawkes Night, the Notting Hill Carnival, and PT Barnum's circus all rolled into one.

I walked back to the hotel, peering in on other restaurants I might sample in the coming days. I made my choices by name more than menu. I'm a sucker for a catchy piece of hoarding. Hence I made a mental note of Mongo's Rock Bottom Café, Restaurant Vegetarianista Lila Vaty, and the wonderfully named Planet Funky Nachos Bar.

I rolled in to the hotel well after hours, largely on account of making a few refuelling stops, first at a steamy, cosy little number called Café Royal down on the main drag, then at Dumbo's, also on the main drag, for a scoop of chirimoya ice cream with papaya and guava sauce and butterscotch puree, and never mind my earlier hectoring on the perils on cholesterol.

Ami and Eyal were in the lobby poring over their right-to-left map. I sat with them a while, shared a cafetiere or two, and discussed the parlous state of the Middle East, playing Jewish geography along the way, only to find that Ami was born and brought up on the self same kibbutz that was home to me for several months back in my days as a post Six-Day War volunteer.

Ami was so thrilled to find a landsman in his midst, he went straight to the hotel's little bar and returned with a bottle of viciously potent Chilean schnapps, or whatever is the South American equivalent, with which to toast our new found kinship.

"I'm afraid I'm not much of a drinker", I said.

A hand or two of gin rummy was suggested.

"I'm not much of a card player either", I protested.

I can be very economical with the truth when it suits - although the not drinking bit is largely true - and it was with bulging pockets and the echo of Hebrew cuss-words ringing in my ears that I hit the sack three hours later.

☙

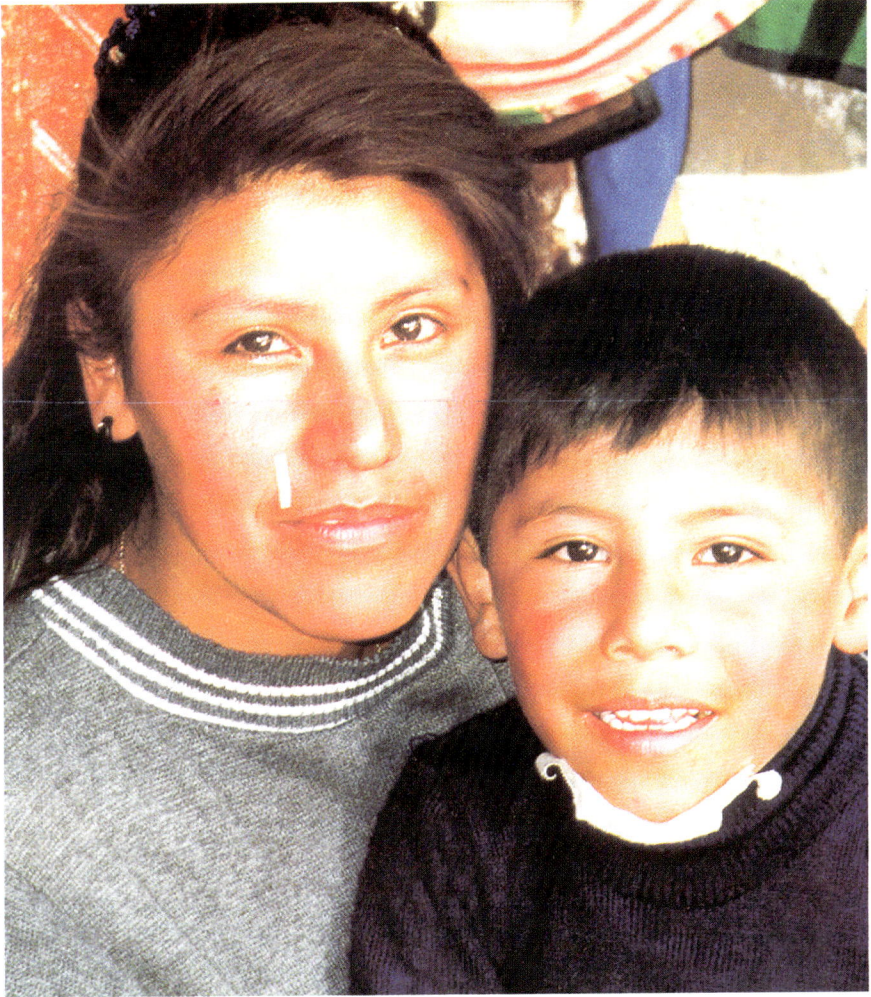

## DIRTY OLD TOWN

Up with the larks, breakfast with a view, and then my morning pick-up. Different guide this time. I'm not sure I caught his name right, but it sounded like Ariel, which sounds suspiciously Israeli for a native Bolivian. Still, that's what it sounded like, so that's what I decided to call him, until corrected.

We wove our way through a riot of madcap colour known as the Friday fruit market. Lorry loads of guava, papaya and chirimoya spilled out into enormous road-side crates, filling every available square centimetre of sidewalk, before filling every micro-millimetre of shopping basket.

What a wonderful, frenzied scene. The old Covent Garden fruit market was never like this, never so ravishingly colourful and sweet-smelling. And never, in all my childhood visits to my favourite old London haunt, did I gorge myself on such an exotic jamboree of fresh fruit, and never mind the madcap speed with which the stuff flies through my system - fast metabolism they call it - and out the other end.

One prolonged toilet stop later, we headed on out of town and up to El Alto, a ramshackle city of unmade roads, open sewers and frequent mud-slides of the most debilitating and damning kind. I wish I could say nice things about El Alto. I don't like speaking ill of a place that is clearly suffering from its own very considerable catalogue of ills. But the best I can say is, if your aim is to visit a place to help bring your social conscience back into sharp focus, El Alto is the place. For this is a city that does its very level best to let you know - and it does so in no uncertain terms - that you've descended, albeit in an upwards direction, from the cosmopolitan metropolis straight into Hell's Kitchen.

Certainly the views from El Alto are staggering, a panorama that unfolds with mounting drama as you emerge from each gaping pothole in the ragbag collection of craters that calls itself a road. The vista, though, did not soft soap me for the reality of the situation. Poverty on a grand scale, with a rainy season that brings with it a raging torrent of human effluent to accompany your every step across this cesspit of a city.

What a dirty, infested, infected

place it is. When you see a garbage truck in El Alto, it's anyone's guess whether it's collecting or delivering. The Incas, they say, spent a fortune developing homesteads in El Alto way back when. Perhaps so. But I'll be damned if it's had so much as a lick of paint since. All the more ironic, then, not to say cruel, that the inhabitants of El Alto, all 700,000 of them, stare full in the face the relative prosperity down in the valley, much the same way as the inmates of Alcatraz used to gaze forlornly over the never-never land of San Fransisco just across the bay. Sometimes life just isn't fair.

El Alto behind us - and in terms of civilization El Alto is behind pretty much everything - we hairpinned and switchbacked yet higher, much higher, 5,000 feet higher, up the mountain, past tiny, translucent tarns, across vast plains of treacherously loose slate, before arriving at Chacaltaya, the world's highest ski resort...though for resort, read lodge, and for lodge, read shed. And for high, read 17,300 feet, which makes the Alps, the Atlas, and Aspen Colorado look positively soppy by comparison.

Nothing in the Alps, not even the runs around Mont Blanc, gets even remotely within black run distance of this dizzyingly high and searingly cold ski summit. In fact, it's only a sub-summit, since the ultimate peak is a further 1,200 feet higher and necessitates a lung-bursting one-in-two haul over a heady mix of depressingly fragile scree and tightly packed glacier. Either way, don't expect to make three forward steps without sliding back two.

But the prize - and what a prize it is - was a view that took away what precious little was left of my breath. La Paz, Illimani, Huayna Potosi, all these places hove into view in one blissful semi-circular sweep. And then, turning full circle, a flash of dazzling azure a way on the horizon that could only have been Lake Titicaca, the jewel, the prince, the entire royal family of all the world's lakes. What a sight.

I scarcely noticed that frostbite was nibbling at my hands and trying its darndest to relieve me of my typing digits. The icicle dangling from my nose was nothing more than a minor irritant, and the manically gale force winds certainly weren't about

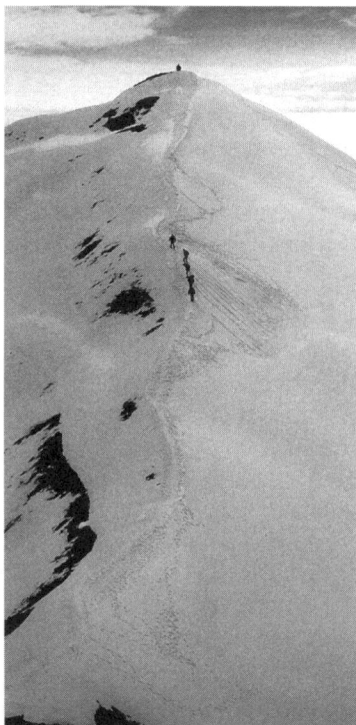

to stop me from purring with pleasure at this white and blue wonderworld. I wasn't about to let the possibility of a hand-free future stop me from sending my camera into overdrive.

What can I tell you? I love mountains. I love everything about them...the way they look, the way they smell, the way they feel, the air, the views, the companionship of fellow climbers, and most of all the sheer challenge just of getting up the bloody things. A townie I may be through and through - and certainly I am the most urban of God's creatures. But without mountains to escape to and hike up, life in the city would be that much poorer.

I asked Ariel if I might be allowed to ski a little. He counselled in favour of caution, and frankly he was right. There is, you see, only one run on Chacaltaya, and that run is blacker than black, the prevailing gradient being the same one-in-two that saw me to the summit. The qualifications for skiing Chacaltaya, it seems, are either extreme skill or a pronounced death wish, and in some cases both. I have neither.

What I do have is a wife and two kids that I'm not particularly keen not to see again, plus a football team who - you'll excuse me if I flatter myself - would be pretty pissed off to lose their rampaging left winger to a fluffy white death. I therefore withdrew my offer to parade my limited panache on this particular mountain in favour of seeing more of the country and more, too, of my family.

So, it was back to La Paz. I dropped off at El Lobo to gorge myself on yet more humus and felafel, and practice my Hebrew on some of the Israeli kids. One told me about the La Paz Seder she went to. 800 people, one of those monster post-Hippy, post-modern, all-welcome, all-included-orthodox-or-not Chabad Lubavitch sing-along Seders that seem these days to seep out of every springtime nook and cranny in every second and third world corner of the globe from Bhutan to Bolivia via Katmandu and Kilimanjaro.

I sat a while longer chatting with the owners of El Lobo, Eli and Dorit Morelli, he a grizzled old veteran of the '82 war in Lebanon who looks uncannily like the bastard love-child of Danny De Vito and Monica Seles, she a native Jewish Bolivian who met Eli in Israel and brought him back to La Paz and who also, it must be said, looks uncannily like the bastard love-child of Danny De Vito and Monica Seles.

Eli and Dorit are wonderful souls, in that soft-centre-beneath-granite-exterior Israeli way, and I was thrilled to bits to be invited that very night to share Kabbalat Shabbat with them and their extended travelling family of carefree little Jewnicks. How could I refuse? An English Jew welcoming in the Sabbath at an Israeli felafel bar in farthest flung Bolivia. That doesn't happen every day. I left El Lobo with much to look forward to.

Back on the street my boots got another going over from an entrepreneurial toddler, buffing up the shine I still had from the earlier going-over. I'm not complaining. I'm very fond of my walking boots and I certainly don't begrudge them a buff and a shine and another going-over every...oh...200 yards or so.

So...I'm yards away from my hotel when I spy something as familiar to me as it is welcome. A gym. I go in. It's basic. Very basic. Hand weights only, no machines, and the very distinct possibility that when the animals walked into the Ark, two by two, so did the weights. But a gym is a gym, and a bicep curl is the same in any language, and at £1 per session an hour passed healthily and cheaply. A shower and mineral water later I felt fresh, relaxed and ready to trade physical for spiritual at Eli and Dorit's Shabbat hoedown.

Well, what can I tell you? Welcoming in the Sabbath at El Lobo was just lovely. Candles were lit, kiddush was made, challa was broken and shared around, Shabbat songs were sung, and in its own easy, relaxed way it was really very moving and very touching. It was a warm, gentle affirmation of my own Jewishness, which I'm always comfortable with, yet somehow has that little bit more meaning halfway across the world and away from my more familiar, and considerably more Jewish, surroundings.

There's something about identifying with your fellow-Jews in far flung places where there's not so many people with whom to identify; something warm and comforting. I don't know if people of other religions do the same. Perhaps it's just a Jewish thing, Jews being by a very long way the least populous of all ethnic minorities, just 14 million of us across the globe. Yet somehow we find each other, as though by radar, and on a Friday night in Bolivia such discovery of kinship gives you a real glow of radiant well-being.

ॐ

## GOD IS IN THE HOUSE

Up before the larks this time. 5 o'clock, that's when I crawled out from under my duvet, and by 5.30 I was out of La Paz, collected and accompanied by Ariel for a dawn drive to Copacabana, down - or should I say up - on the shores of Lake Titicaca. I say up because, unbelievably, Titicaca sits way up at 13,000 feet above sea level, by far the highest navigable lake in the world. Picture it; a lake as high in the sky as almost any peak in the Atlas mountains, and more than most in the Alps...and the Andes, for that matter. The mind boggles, especially for an altitude anorak like me.

I like journeying at dawn. You know sunrise is just around the corner, and as the sun comes up amid the peace and solitude of the empty open road, you feel as though you really are the lord of all you survey. With bucolic vistas all around and Nick Cave droning through my headphones - I think he was singing "God is in The House", which seemed entirely appropriate in the circumstances - the day could not possibly have dawned in a more inspiring way.

We drove the open road until we reached the narrowest point in the lake. From there we crossed the lake in a small motor boat from San Pedro to San Pablo, while our bus floated alongside on the deck of a large bus-carrying barge. Ten minutes later we reached the other side, having saved ourselves, I was told, the better part of the six hours it would have taken to drive the cumbersome mountain roads that skirt around that particular stretch of lake.

We continued along the isthmus that all but splits the lake in two, Bolivia to one side, Peru to the other, until our eyes feasted on a wee little town down by the water's edge, nestling between two piton-like pinnacles and centred around an elaborately mosaic-embossed cathedral which I could tell, even from this distance, was an edifice of rare and unique beauty. This was Copacabana.

I dumped my stuff (why do I always say that? I'm no dumper; I'm a fold neatly and putter awayer) in Room 107 of the Residencial Rosario and made straight for the cathedral.

Now I'm not a religious man, but opportunities to witness the ritual blessing by the local padre of a score and more new and semi-new Toyotas come, like truthful statements from Jeffrey Archer, perhaps once in a lifetime. The ceremony is simple, cerebral, and supremely silly. A prayer is said car-side by the cathedral steps, holy water (GTX I presume) is sprinkled on each of the flower-festooned bonnets, and the cars are then driven the hundred metres or so to the lakeside for...I really can't believe I'm about to say this, but it's true, I assure you...for Baptism, following which they are deemed ready and able to tackle the network of slalom courses, dodgem rides, and pock-marked dirt tracks masquerading loosely, and not altogether convincingly, as Bolivian highways.

Ariel asked if I'd witnessed such a thing before. "I'm Jewish", I replied. "We don't baptize our cars, we circumcise them. Two inches off the exhaust, a dab of kosher wine, then seven times around the local shopping mall". An old gag to be sure; but in Copacabana, a whole new audience.

This was one for the archives. I popped into the Alf@Net Internet Café down along the main drag to send home intelligence of this bizarre spectacle, but more importantly to pick up a particular soccer score from a particular soccer team down in the nether reaches of the English football league. The café is run by a really nice English couple - Copacabana is full of northern hemisphere settlers who came, fell in love, and settled - and I was delighted to be offered free access any time I wanted to their pool table and video collection, which was commendably short on blockbusters and blissfully long on Coen Brothers and Woody Allen.

Out in the garden of the adjoining Colonial Hostal I bumped into the embassy guys from Day One, plus some other young Sabras from last night at El Lobo. Together we set off for a hike up the larger of the two pitons, the Cerro Calvario. The ascent was by way of an old Inca staircase of the knee-wrenching

variety I'd first encountered on Peru's fabled Inca Trail, the kind where each step rises some 20 inches and reduces the backs of your knees to a painfully tender mass of strained sinews and trembling tendons.

It was worth it. The views from the top were achingly beautiful, across the lake and into Peru, across the town and beyond to the mountains that huddle and then stretch the length and breadth of the horizon. I headed back down the Cerro with the most perfect of pictures burnt into my mind. It was very, very lovely.

Back in the garden of the Colonial Hostal I ran into a couple of colourful characters. The first was Leanne, a travel photographer from New Orleans whose family, like mine, derives from the little Dutch seaside town of Scheveningen. Leanne, who was travelling with her teenage daughter, showed me her camera, a really hi-tech and quite baffling affair with a hundred and one attachments, each one higher-tech and more baffling than the next. I didn't understand a bit of it. I'm no technological genius, admittedly. In fact, my fecklessness when faced with anything more complicated than the common light switch is the stuff of legends around the Moss household. But I swear to God, even David Bailey would need a finely detailed and illustrated user's manual to help unravel the mysteries of Leanne's equipment. And were her photos any better than mine? Well...actually, yes, they were.

Leanne was a big girl, a real big girl, in that real big all-American real big girl kind of a way, the kind of girl whose bottom, if the screen broke down at your local drive-in movie, would make a more than adequate replacement. She was also wonderfully, uninhibitedly forward in that Dr. Joyce Brothers-meets-Dr. Ruth Westerheimer-at-the-Betty-Ford-Clinic-and-discusses-the-joys-of-frigidity-with-a-roomful-of-recovering-alcholic-nuns kind of a way.

"So, how much do you earn?" she asked me, as a prelude to "what's your name?" and "where are you from?" Without so much as drawing breath she launched herself into the more-information-than-anyone-would-want overdrive that Americans you've only just met do so well.

"You'll never guess who I balled when I was covering the last R.E.M. tour", she announced. The whole band, I shouldn't wonder, and probably at the same time. There's certainly enough of her to go around. Not that I said any of this to her. I was too busy with my mental visualization of Michael Stipe and the female equivalent of the Hindenburg.

"I balled Jim Morrison back in '67", she confided. "And Hendrix, and those guys from ZZ Top. All those dead guys - I balled them, every last one". So that's what killed them, I thought, as I looked in awe at this voluminous office block of a woman and her very petite, very beautiful daughter.

Leanne - who, I rapidly came to realise, was almost indistinguishable from Tony Soprano - proceeded to share with me her entire life story. She led me on a tour from her first post-high school assignment trailing and photographing Malcolm X, via the Waco Texas Massacre, all the way to the latest Bush inauguration, and most points in between, including her induction into travel photography, which only happened in the first place on account of her getting thrown off the R.E.M. tour and having nothing left to photograph in Nevada but desert landscapes.

She also told me about how she took two or three months out of her schedule to become a primal therapist, which I believe entails the exchanging of much verbal abuse with people of high-velocity temperament and copious wallets, which covers pretty much most Americans and for which Leanne, as she herself freely admits, is paid a not immoderate king's ransom. She offered me a free session, but what with my Kabbalah and salsa lessons, to say nothing of my post-graduate degree course in feng shui, acupuncture and tantric sex, I graciously declined her generous offer to have my flabby larynx and sagging life toned up.

What a girl Leanne was. I'd have gladly exchanged bodily fluids with her, but such was her immensity I fear my modest offering would have gone unnoticed.

Then there was Alex, a reluctantly Jewish former Soviet refusenik who, if I didn't know better, and therefore know well enough how Russian Jews all look exactly the same, I'd have seriously thought I might have met back in the 80s when I was doing my human rights bit in Moscow and Leningrad. Alex holed up a while in Jerusalem, once he eventually got his exit visa from that nice Mr. Gorbachev, before sampling the pure, undiluted joys of freedom by travelling the world in general, South America in particular, and Bolivia in all of its finest detail.

Alex and I swapped notes on anything and everything, from Buddhism to Kabbalah, Kafka to the Marx Brothers, and Marrakech to Bergen, where, apparently, he is keen to lay down his knapsack for a while and settle down with a flaxen-haired strumpet called Ingrid Guudjonnssonn. I couldn't recommend Bergen highly enough. It's one of my favourite towns and I have little doubt that it will soon, what with my endorsement and Alex's evident wanderlust, be welcoming him to its copious Nordic bosom.

Alex and I talked for hours - with so much in common it was very easy - and I had this warm feeling that seems to come whenever I share prime time with a kindred spirit. My afternoon with Alex was illuminating and, in its own way, really quite uplifting, and it only added to the general sense of well being that travel brings me.

Goodness me, but I'm sounding a tad philosophical for a simple country boy. Better I get into list-making mode, namely the nationalities of fellow-trekkers as perceived from conversations picked up and observations made by yours truly. In doing so I offer no guarantees as to accuracy, and absolutely no favouritism towards the Dutch, who are superb travellers and probably my favourite people, or the

## PLACES BEGINNING WITH 'B'

British, who are neither. Here goes...

1. Israeli
2. American
3. German
4. French
5. Dutch
6. Australian/New Zealand ...whatever, antipodean
7. Canadian
8. Swedish
9. Everyone else
10. Israeli (2$^{nd}$ appearance, on account of there are so damn many!)

and finally...unclassified...British, for whom Ibiza and Aiya Napa would apparently still seem to present the boozier, more mindless we're-here-for-the-beer-and-chips option.

And with that I strolled back to Room 107 for a bath and a change of undies, before heading down to the lake, through the hotel's back garden, to snap sunset over Titicaca. And what a sunset it was, an aurora borealis of colour sent by the heavens to play on the lake, before sending me haring like a mad thing up those fecking great Inca steps to the top of Calvario for some seriously top notch photographs on my humble little idiot-proof camera.

Four days gone, eight rolls of film done, forty shots per film. The mathematics are simple, work it out for yourselves. All I can say is, moderation has no place in the life and times of the itinerant traveller and his Olympus Zoom 70 pocket camera.

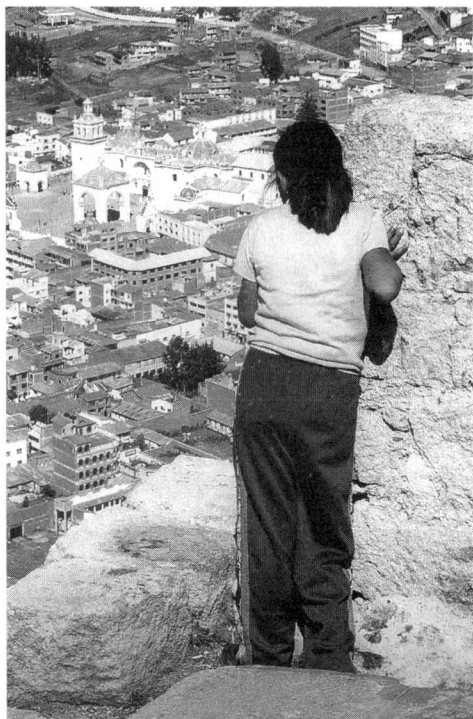

Ah well, back to the hotel for a spot of supper. I sat myself by the lake-facing window and readied myself for a meal that might do justice to a quite ravenous appetite, brought on by all those physical and verbal exertions of the previous few hours. I was told the Titicaca trout is by far the best option around these parts. It is. It slid down a treat, as indeed did I, under my bedding, for a thumping good nights sleep and the very real prospect of the mother of all views to wake up to in the morning.

$\infty$

## AN ISLAND IN THE SUN

With a room facing full-on to the lake, the mother of all views is precisely what I woke up to. With three hours to kill before being collected, I was up and at it, packed and breakfasted within minutes. The sun's hat was at a jaunty angle and I wanted to get to the main square just as quickly as I could.

It was Sunday, I was in deeply superstitious Catholic country, and I wanted another look at the Toyotas in all their finery, trussed up and ready for a hard days blessing. And there they were, in all their flowery splendour; bumpers, wipers, windshields and roof racks all but submerged in a sea of carnations, gladioli and lilies of the valley. What a sight to behold.

And there we were, me and the lass from New Orleans, to catch the chassis confirmation on our respective cameras, she fumbling with enough lenses and tripods to open a department store, me with one hand on my Zoom, the other nonchalantly adjusting my Ray-Bans.

Religiously speaking the ceremony makes enormous sense. We Jews lose two inches off our todgers, based on some sort of badly drawn covenant between Abraham and God, so why shouldn't the Catholics sprinkle a little water, say a few Hail Marys, and kid themselves they now own a car that either of the Schumacher boys would be proud to own. Mind you, Bolivia does have the highest death-by-driving rate in South America, if not world-wide, so maybe they should cut the baptism and stick to a good old-fashioned bris. It would certainly make the car lighter, if a little less sensitive to human touch.

The whole thing was great fun, festive and colourful, though such was the bitching, bellyaching and hair-pulling over who saw what parking space first, to say nothing of the double-parking, it's hard to believe these people weren't Jewish.

I met Hernan - at last I discovered Ariel's real name, and the perceptive amongst you might notice how completely dissimilar the two names are - and together we headed for the harbour to board the comfy, velvet-seated Transturin 15-passenger catamaran bound for Isla del Sol.

We were served lunch almost as soon as we boarded. Gourmet stuff, very Marco Pierre White, and frankly far too rich and unsubtle for me this early in the day. I left that to the others - eight leathery septugenarians and a young Japanese girl who was eyeing me in that inscrutable Japanese way that suggests either distaste or lust or, it's entirely possible, both. I was keen to find out. I quite fancied my chances here. I was in no hurry, though. I was happy enough to go up top, take the air and admire the sheer wonder of the lake - the turquoise water, the rugged cliffs, the rolling hills, the whole package that is Titicaca.

An hour went by very quickly before we docked at Yumani and hopped a reed boat to Isla del Sol, the fabled Sun Island, for a hike up an Inca staircase to the island's main viewpoint. What a lovely hike it was, gentle rather than challenging, with the most glorious views opening out as we went.

We eased our way up and over Balinese-like crop terraces, past grazing alpaca and Shetland-sized ponies, amid row upon row of flowering shrubs and sprouting herbs. And all the way we were accompanied, whether we liked it or not, by a battalion of wide-eyed kids, for whom scamming a penny or two posing for photographs presented a far better option than life in the schoolroom.

At one plateau we saw an demonstration of reed boat making, at another we were regaled by an exposition of Inca history, and at the island's very highest point, a couple of hundred metres above the water's edge, we witnessed - in fact were part of - a very nice little ceremony as performed by the local shamen, which ended in each of us being blessed by the chief priest.

In one fell swoop, bedecked in a floral garland and sprinkled with holy water, I knew what it was like to be a Toyota. OK, so being baptized is, how shall I say, not quite ecumenically sound for the proverbial nice Jewish boy. And certainly I'd have been forgiven at that moment for digging into my backpack, retrieving my mobile phone, and calling up my rabbi for his considered view on the matter.

But I wasn't about to complain. I was cleansed, spiritually and literally, and went back down the mountain smelling of roses; and the whole exercise rendered me, if only in Bolivian terms, every bit as fast, and probably a good deal more reliable, than any Japanese motor on the open Bolivian road.

Back on the catamaran I made straight for the sun deck…and that was it for next ninety minutes. One minute I'm being moved closer to Christ, the next I'm giving myself as some sort of kosher offering to the sun. And what a place to do it. Lake Titicaca presents a magical sight. A huge expanse of water it might be; but so many are the islands that dot the translucent waters along the way, there is virtually no point on the lake at which land is not visible to the naked eye, be it crop terraces or snow-capped mountains. Grasmere is pretty, Maggiori is romantic, and Lake Bled is so photogenic you could earn a fortune selling your snaps as postcards. But Titicaca wins the cigar. It is spellbindingly gorgeous.

It was good sitting out under a sun that seemed to add a good twenty degrees to the temperature, and I'd have gladly sat out until the sun went down over the lake. Alas my tanning time was limited, and we docked soon after five and headed straight back by road for La Paz. I was delighted to get a room ending in 07 at the El Rey Palace, 607 this time. 07 rooms, you see, are not just rooms, but fully fledged suites with city *and* mountain views...nice enough by day, unbelievable by night, La Paz resembling a discount lighting warehouse after dark.

I dropped my stuff in 607 and headed out to El Lobo for a felafel supper, before slip-sliding back in the rain for a squint at the late film on HBO, and a rummage through my Spanish pocket dictionary for the odd useful phrase or two. I didn't bother looking up the word *gutter*. It seemed a pointless exercise. La Paz, you see, doesn't have any, not that I could see anyway, hence the streets flood with quite alarming ferocity after just a twenty minute downpour, leaving me ever so slightly miffed at having restricted my travelling footwear, walking boots aside, to a flimsy pair of sandals.

I wonder how *galoshes* translates.

&#x2767;

## CAMP, CRAMP AND CRAMPONS

Last night was not a good night. I woke up so many times, going to bed in the first place seemed as futile as Bill Clinton swotting up on the vows of fidelity. The reason? Rampant runs, a very wet and wobbly tummy. The cause? Well, I doubt it was the falafel - Middle Eastern food and I are rarely in disagreement - so I can only guess it was falling asleep on the sun deck of the catamaran under the searing sun without a sun hat. And just how stupid is that, especially to one so follically challenged?

I stumbled down to breakfast, a blinding headache now on board, and treated the buffet table like some kind of minefield, picking and choosing my breakfast by what may least annoy an already extremely pissed off tummy. I settled on a cup of Coca tea and...er...that was it.

Freddie - he was my guide for the half-week mountain trek - collected me at 8.30 and I was introduced to my fellow trekkers, a late 30s couple from Portland Oregon, she clearly Jewish, he clearly not. I gathered this much, aside from visual appearances, by his being an avid weekend trekker who referred to his grandmother as Grammy, and her wearing the kind of bemused what-the-fuck-am-I-doing-here expression that Jewish girls in the wilds do so well.

Their names were a bit of a giveaway too, he Chuck, she Rivka. I'm not stereotyping here, you understand, but you tell me, how many Jewish Chucks did you ever hear of? And, for that matter, when was the last time...think long and hard now, this is a serious question of great ethnic sensitivity...when was *absolutely* the last time you ran into a goyische girl called Rivka? I'll tell you when. Never. They don't exist, not unless conceived by a couple with a highly developed sense of irony, which in America, you have to admit, is pretty damn unlikely.

The drive through the early morning drizzle to La Cumbre was...well...drizzly, but where we set down our jeep to commence our upwards slog was dramatic and thrilling. As we stepped out into the snow at 14,000 feet a condor circled above us, casting his beady eye on the interlopers in his domain. And as I looked up at the 3,000 feet of altitude gain that we were to tackle before lunch, I was all but consumed with child-like excitement, a feeling that barely dampened on Freddie announcing what was on our after-lunch agenda - a further five hours and a further 7,000 feet - down this time - to our first nights camp. Now *this* was to look forward to.

The climbing was sublime, crampon and glacier in holy union, and in no time at all we'd hit the summit. I looked down in awe, the sky now perfectly clear, a wide open window to the land below. Wispy wafts of cloud rose from the river, way, way down on the bed of the valley, while birds of prey surfed the thermals so close to us we could almost reach out and touch them. The whole setting was truly mystical.

In such surroundings we savoured a leisurely picnic lunch, before beginning our long, languid descent. I walked for an hour or so on my own in heavenly silence, then with Rivka, and then with Freddie, with whom I discussed everything from healthcare, or lack of, in Bolivia, to the parlous state Cuba might find itself in should Castro ever curl up his toes and join the choir invisible. Don't ask me why Cuba. It's a favourite topic, a political hobby horse, part of my latent Red Period which I seem to go through every time America elects a gun-loving, good ol' boy, right wing redneck of a president, hell-bent on obliterating worldwide threats, which somehow only they can see, to the greater good of mankind, American oil revenues, and the next presidential election....not that I'm cynical.

Eventually - 6.30 - we reached our camp site, free of any bumps, bruises or broken bones, which is no mean feat, let me tell you, on such treacherously slippery downhill terrain. The setting was idyllic, the river meandering through a camp site sheltered by hills and crags, half-lost in a dreamy haze of low level mist, the whole thing oddly reminiscent, of all things, of the good old Scottish Cairngorms.

After the abdominal trials and tribulations of the early-morning, I approached supper with a degree of circumspection and settled on what seemed the most sensible course of action. I didn't have any. Instead I hit the sack at 7.30 aiming for a straight eleven hours sleep, if only to beat last night's effort by ten hours.

## NEGOTIATING JEFF BRIDGES

My Wish came true. I got my eleven hours. I woke up with a clear head, stable bowels, and a quite uncommonly huge appetite, which I greedily satisfied with two bowls of steaming hot porridge, an intemperately huge battery of sugared pancakes and jam, and a Spanish omelette of such immensity the only plate on which it might reasonably be accommodated is the huge silver one they give the Ladies champion each summer at Wimbledon. And you wonder why my tummy gets upset.

I woke up also to a fabulous dawn vista and a sun unfeasibly strong for so early an hour. This was a day to look forward to, and I just couldn't wait to get out there and mix it with the mountains and streams of the High Cordillera. My tummy felt good, my legs felt strong, I was ready to trek.

Well, the trekking was glorious - tough, but not too tough, say Kilimanjaro Day Four. We bumbled and stumbled our slippery way through the rain forest, emerging alongside the length of river that bisects the jungle, the snowy peaks of yesterday poking through the overhang. And when we turned half circle we gawped in amazement as the steam rose from the swampy rain forest across the valley, fairly obliterating the snow peaks of the Andes, before melting into the sky a mile or two above our heads.

We wended our way up the mountain, peeling layers of clothing as we went, right down to T-shirts and shorts. No danger of nasty biting insects here. Just flocks of butterflies, every colour of the rainbow, and avenues of hulking great rubber plants oozing latex like so many litres of correcting fluid.

We lunched under the sun on avocado, tomatoes and goats cheese, before crossing the river on the ropiest rope bridge you ever saw, one at a time as it was evidently in danger of imminent collapse, before scaling a thousand feet or so of achingly steep Inca steps to reach our reward, a view of the never climbed Tikimani, all 20,000 feet of it. It was spectacular. And the occasion, I'm afraid, got to my bowels.

I hurriedly found myself a little hidey-hole, grabbed my loo roll, and did what a man has to do, crapping in full view of an unclimbed mountain, whilst at the same time creating my own not insignificant unclimbed mountain, and both of them with steam rising from the foothills. A small step for man, a slippery one for whoever was bringing up the rear.

Rivka and Chuckie - that's what she called him, Chuckie - mixed me a post-diarrhoea herbal drink. They're into all that herbal stuff. Healthy living fairly oozed from their every New Age orifice. He's a nature photographer, it turns out, and she runs a health food, meditation and colonic irrigation drop-in centre. The Buddhist Bagel, I think it was called, or maybe it was The Internal Washout Company. Whatever, they were as syrupy and saint-like a pair of individuals as ever I met, and together they had that winsome air of gooey lovey-doveyness that can only suggest divorce is imminent. No-one can be that in love without really hating one another; it has to be an act....not that I'm cynical.

Trekking with Rivka and Chuckie was like walking with God, or if not God, then at the very least Cliff Richard and Mother Theresa. I swear to Jesus these people could fuck like rabbits and still wind up virgins. What a pair. Caring Chuckie and his butterfly photos, and ravishing Rivka with her sandalwood scented tampons and environment-friendly orgasms.

These guys were way, *way* more good than too good to be true, and I truly didn't know what I'd done to deserve them. And when I looked a little more closely at their backpacks and saw a golden furry head poking out of each...well...I just knew God was alive and well and taking the piss. They only had matching teddy bears! How twee is that? I could have chucked all over Chuckie and Rivka right there and then.

Up and down mountainsides we went, teddy bears in tow, over rope bridges, log bridges, Jeff Bridges, sometimes wading through the river, clambering down extremely muddy mud banks and over unfeasibly huge boulders, before reaching our hilltop campsite with just enough daylight to take in the full beauty of our surroundings. The campsite, in essence, was a narrow ledge, the width of three or four tents at the most, with the jungle way down the one side, a thundering river way down the other, and a whopping great tureen of pasta in between and ready for consumption by Mr. Cynical Bastard and Mr. and Mrs. Two-Teddies-In-Tow.

The setting was wondrous and morning could not come soon enough. I couldn't wait to watch the sun rise over this visual, verdant paradise, and I went to sleep with a sky full of stars firmly imprinted on my mind, and the sound, I swear to God, of lullabys from the next tent.

"Please, God", I thought to myself. "Tell me these people aren't actually *singing* to their teddies. That would be too much to bear. And please, God, if they are singing to their teddies, make them suffer with extreme prejudice, unorganically if possible".

And with that little prayer, I drifted into a slumberous state, blissfully unconcerned at the distinct possibility that I might, in the dead of the night, find myself responsible for the savage dismembering and wholesale mutilation of a pair of fluffy, cuddly, golden brown creatures...and perhaps even the teddies.

## THERE'S A NIP IN THE AIR

Woken at 6 by a brace of hormonal cockerels, I jumped out of the tent - and on such a narrow ledge, very nearly off the mountain - to catch the sun rise over the Andes. It was beautiful. I looked in awe at the day that was laid out before me, a 25 kilometre hike up and down hills and valleys, the full extent of which was just a little too distant to glimpse through sleep-filled eyes.

We breakfasted al fresco, together with a mini-United Nations of trekkers, late night mountain-top arrivals from yesterday - one Dutch, one Brazilian, one Taiwanese, and, remarkably enough, no Israelis. Parrots and condors circled overhead in unlikely harmony, the porridge was commendably lump-free, and I could tell we were in for a good day, perhaps even a memorable day...for today we were off to see The Japanese Man.

Let me tell you about The Japanese Man.

The story is, he fled industrially-ravaged post-War Japan in the early-fifties, settling first in La Paz, then moving ever outward from the city in search of real solitude, away from what you and I might term civilization, eventually fetching up on an isolated hilltop 17,000 feet up the Andes. From 1960 until today he's lived alone. No people. Just dogs, frogs, sheep and horses, all of which he breeds, it is said, for eating purposes; dogs legs and frogs legs al dente. And we were off to find him.

Striding to the top of the region's highest waterfall, the water thundered heaven knows how many hundreds of feet to the basement of this particular pass. We walked the Inca staircase down the mountain, criss-crossing the river over rope bridges, some with just the one log to balance on over torrential waters, before reaching a watering hole straight of that gorgeous scene with the dusky maidens in *O Brother Where Art Thou*. Such unimaginable, dream-like tranquility.

We continued back up the mountain to the Chucura Pass at 16,000 feet, back down again through numerous altitude and climate zones, all signs of civilization banished to dim and distant memory. Back up we went again, higher this time than before; so high, in fact, we were above the cloud line and in the full glare of the blazing noonday sun. God was in the house - that much was apparent even to the staunchest sceptic in his realm - and how appropriate that it was the song of that name that ran through my mind, Nick Cave's dulcet tones filling my head once more, as it had done so many times on my Bolivian journey.

For a moment out there I was Captain Willard closing in on Colonel Kurtz in *Apocalypse Now*. There I was, on the trail of the legendary hermit, Japan's answer to Robinson Crusoe, way up high in his own tiny kingdom above the clouds in the Bolivian Andes. And, like Captain Willard going up river in search of Kurtz, I could sense I was close. Actually, I could see I was close, for on rounding a corner at the crest of the next ridge, there on a hilltop stood - perhaps that should be perched - a tin-roofed, mud-walled, all-but-decomposing house. It had to be his, as The Japanese Man's assemblage of flimsy materials masquerading as a house is the only such structure - a term I use as loosely as whoever built his home wielded their tools - for many a mountain and many a mile.

And then I was there.

I scampered across to his homestead and was greeted by a wizened old fellow in tatty Ban-The-Bomb T-shirt and even tattier baseball cap. He spotted the Star of David around my neck and spoke to me in flawless Hebrew. I was impressed. He showed me his estate. I was more impressed. No running water, no electricity, no drainage, no sewage, no mirrors - imagine not knowing what you've looked like for forty-odd years - and yet, for all that, the finest view on Earth, across the steamy groves of the Yungas, over rain forest and waterfalls, to the snow-capped peak of the unclimbed Tikimani. Perhaps he'll be the first to climb it.

The house is so prehistoric it's almost *pre*-prehistoric. And yet, in its own way - surrounded by flowers and cacti, valleys and forests, and big, big mountains - it is idyllic, bucolic, and quite mesmerisingly peaceful. I doubt I could live like that, in such isolation. Personally I'd miss my local café, the London Film Festival, the Eurosport Channel. And who would I play football with? And who, for that matter, would get the ball every time it missed the net and flew down the mountain?

But the Japanese Man seems happy enough, blissfully happy if truth be told, on the rooftop of the Andes, and if he's chosen not once to venture forth from his mountain for close on half-a-century, then who am I to argue the case for urban mayhem? And anyway, as for his being a hermit...well...I'm not so sure about that. I met him, Rivka and Chuckie met him, and the guys from Holland, Brazil and Taiwan met him. In fact - and get this - he even has a visitors book, top heavy with Israelis of course, which explains, I guess, the flawless Hebrew.

At a rough count, taking our time with him as an average kind of visiting day, I'd say he must get hundreds of visitors each year, which, as hermits go, puts him rather closer to the social league of Peter Stringfellow and Ivana Trump than Howard Hughes and Lord Lucan. No-one, it seems, does the Choro trek without dropping in for tea and frogs on Mr. Tamiji Hanamura de Furio.

I'm pleased I met him. We didn't converse much, but he was so happy to conjoin me to pore over his collection of maps, the relative newness of which was in such strange contrast to the likes of his bed - two planks of wood and a sliver of raffia

matting - and the holes in the wall where one might have expected to see doors and windows, to say nothing of a collection of enough stuffed animals and other assorted debris and detritus - to suggest I'd wandered up the mountain and into a Damien Hirst show. This guy could earn a fortune.

Our time in the Japanese quarter done, we fairly sprinted the 6,000 foot drop to the tiny hillside hamlet of Chairo that brought our trek to a close, just in time for some fresh baked bread and pastries at the local store, before jumping on the back of the open camion that would carry us to Coroico along the Yungas Road.

Ah, the Yungas Road, the insanely dangerous road that slithers and snakes its 10,000 foot descent from La Cumbre to Coroico, flirting capriciously with disaster along the way. This road is so ludicrously dangerous they should close it down, except it's so damn exciting. Take it from me, there is one huge adrenaline rush in riding the back of an open truck on a road where waterfalls cascade across your unsurfaced path with such force as to erode the euphemistically-called highway before your very eyes. Look up and monolithic great rocks overhang the cars that dare to take to the road. Look down - which is all too easy on a road with one lane and no safety barriers - and your nose will bleed in tune to the sheer 3,000 foot drops to some distant place the other side of Hades.

Fatal accidents, they say, are edging ever closer to one a week on Suicide Alley. All those pretty roadside flowers along the way? Look closer. They're wreaths. Fasten your belt, place your faith in Jesus, prostrate yourself to the God of broken crankshafts, and take to the open (but for how much longer) road. That's what I did, all except the Jesus bit, and I got to Coroico safe and sound and pretty damn keen to find a toilet.

Freddie booked me a seat on the bus for tomorrow's ride back to La Paz, before he and I and the cuddly, fluffy teddy bears, all four of them, said our respective goodbyes. I checked myself into the Hotel Gloria, a fusty, musty, sadly forlorn hostelry whose better days were surely in the dim and distant pre-electricity and telecommunications age. Cold water only in the shower - apart from an absudly huge spider, that is - but I didn't care. I was so caked in dirt I'd have gladly shared my tub with anything with eight legs. Cameron Diaz and her three sisters come to mind.

It was with a jaunty step and a dead spider on the sole of my boot that I made it up the hill to the village square for a spot of supper and another of Bolivia's neon sunset views, across the horizon to the distant 20,000 footers of the High Andes. It was tough to say what Coroico was like, but that's what tomorrows are for when you're on the road.

&#8239;&#8239;&#8239;&#8239;&#8239;&#8239;&#8239;&#8239;&#8239;&#8239;&#8239;&#8239;&#8239;&#8239;&#8239;&#8239;&#8239;&#8239;&#8239;&#8239;&#8239;&#8239;&#8239;&#8239;&#8239;&#8239;&#8239;&#8239;&#8239;&#8239;&#8239;&#8239;&#8239;&#8239;&#8239;&#8239;&#8239;&#8239;&#8239;&#8239;cs

## MAKE SURE YOU WEAR CLEAN UNDERWEAR

Woken - whether I liked it or not - by a somewhat avant garde mix of crowing cockerels, howling coyote, and Freddie Mercury singing "I Want to be Free" (I'll take the cockerels and the coyote, thank you very much). Still, it was 8.30, I'd slept the better part of ten hours, so no complaints. I looked out of the window, keen to judge Coroico by daylight. Nothing doing. Coroico was so completely shrouded in mist, I might just as well have been staring into a bowl of Friar's Balsam. Visual impressions would have to be put on hold a while longer.

Once dressed and in the hotel's reception I made a startling and sobering discovery. Of all the establishment's forty or so rooms, Room 6, the one I was in, had clearly been the only one occupied last night. Every other key was up there on the rack, and the reception area had the air of a sinking ship just after all the rats had scampered away and deserted. Even the receptionist was nowhere to be found.

Two distinct possibilities existed. Either America had just invaded Coroico, or this was the least popular hostelry in the whole of Bolivia. Whatever, I wasn't about to hang around to find out. I put my key up on the rack, left a $20 bill and a hand-written note on the reception desk, and wandered up the hill to the little town square to find out if I was indeed the last person left on the face of the Earth.

I needn't have worried. I found plenty of people, more than enough to remind me I was back in the land of the living, and all of them in the German run Back-Stube Konditorei, a diner that would more than hold its own in a trendy corner of Greenwich Village. The food was wonderful, just wonderful - fresh, home-made, and quite ridiculously tasty, from the yoghurts and pancakes to the muffins and strudels, via a bewildering selection of coffees from every corner of the coffee-making globe.

It was 9.30 and every last place setting was taken, with almost everyone plumping for the apparently legendary muesli, which was so rich in fresh fruits you could plant a tree in the middle of the bowl and call it an orchard. I ate myself into submission and still asked for more.

The everyone I refer to comprised, to a man and woman, travellers and trekkers. Seasoned, itinerant travellers and trekkers. Some, like me, were on the road for a month or two, some rather longer, while one guy, perhaps a little older than me, was in the middle of a nine month break from the real world of second mortgages and performance-related bonuses back in his Dublin-based merchant bank.

I know people back home who regard this kind of mid-life hiatus as somewhat capricious, not to say reckless. I don't understand that. We only go round once, and to my way of thinking it's downright reckless *not* to do it. The rat race is only ever won by the rats, and sometimes you have to know when to take a prolonged break, and if your wife, husband or partner doesn't understand, just keep e-mailing from Kazakhstan, or Tierra Del Fuego, or wherever you happen to fetch up, until they do understand. A man works 35 years, give him a break.

Life on the road is essential food for the soul - this soul at least - especially when the soul resides for the most part in the big, smoky city, a philosophy shared by the guy from Dublin, who had just arrived in Bolivia following a sojourn jaguar-spotting in Paraguay, and a somewhat lengthier stint living amongst the Mennonites of northern Chile. His name was Sean, and together, over countless cappuccinos, Sean and I swapped notes on Belize, Ecuador, the Galapagos Islands, and wherever else we'd both found ourselves these past months. I was very happy.

After breakfast I popped next door to Artesania, the handicraft and folklore store owned by the café people, to buy frankincense and myrrh for the folks back home. It was mid-morning and the sun was beating the little square to a steamy pulp. It seemed a fine place to sit, write, contemplate, and chew the fat with whoever was knocking around, which is just what I did until I was ready to pull out of town.

This, it would seem, is the major activity in Coroico. Sitting, schmoozing, and pulling out of town, interspersed with the odd bowl of muesli. Coroico is the original one-horse town, and when the horse saddles up and mosies on out it must be mighty hard to think what to do in this sleepy little backwater. But then, after a tough few days trekking in the mountains, nothing is as good a thing to do as anything.

Coroico nailed in a morning, it was with huge anticipation - mostly excitement with a soupcon of dread - that I left this jungle-top perch on board an ancient and decidedly dodgy looking minibus for the complete Yungas road trip back to La Paz. Yesterday, hors d'ouvres; today, main course, dessert, and after-dinner wafer thin mints.

I asked the driver what condition the road was in, like I didn't know. "Fantastico!" he replied, without blushing, sweating, or batting an eyelid in the way inveterate liars usually do. And it was a quite monumental whopper of a fib, given the Yungas Road is a death trap at the best of times. But let's face it, he doesn't want to lose customers before he gets the chance to *really* lose customers, if you get my meaning.

Well, the Yungas ride, the full monty Yungas ride, is extraordinary. More dangerous - *way* more dangerous - than yesterday's taster would have had me believe, the road so crudely scarred and cripplingly eroded, you could dig a metre-deep trench the width of the so-called highway in twenty minutes flat with a teaspoon and a pair of nail-clippers.

It's a curious phenomenon of the Yungas Road that everyone who rides it, from what I could see, is gloriously cavalier about the whole thing, almost willing the bus to do a Titanic and submerge itself in the murkiest of depths way down the near-vertical mountainside. Of course, there's always an exception to the rule, and it's just my luck that she was sitting next to me, rocking back and forth, her lips mouthing what I can only surmise was the Spanish equivalent of The Lord's Prayer, or possibly a rehearsal of Kaddish, her shoulders quivering with what I have latterly come to recognise as Tim-Henman-at-matchpoint terror.

To be fair - and I say this notwithstanding my own well-practised bravura - the lady had a point. The Yungas Road is - and this is something that must surely be beyond all reasonable doubt - the original source of numerous expressions from "sailing close to the wind" to "taking a free drop". At no time on the 4-hour journey were we any further than 12 miserly inches from the precipitous edge, and when we were forced to make way - this is a single track road, don't forget, and never mind the highway bit - for the mother of all articulated lorries, I swear to God we were, at most, at the very, very most, *three* inches from dropping to eternity, eternity in this case being the dense Yungas jungle thousands of feet below. Madness, sheer madness.

And nothing was more stir crazy than finding ourselves the target of a rapid succession of roadside waterfalls, as they spilled their all on our humble, and almost certainly unblessed, Toyota from a very great height. This wasn't driving, this was white water rafting.

What a journey. My nails turned white, my hair turned grey - well, it would have done if I had any - and I'm only grateful I was wearing the right colour briefs. It's moments like this when you appreciate the efficacy of you mother exhorting you all those years ago to wear clean underwear. I always wondered why she said this. Now I know. Thanks Mum. Take a Bolivian ride; I'd like to return the advice.

We docked in La Paz at around 5.30 and it was back to my home away from home, the warm and welcoming El Rey Palace. Up to Room 507 I went, my main luggage and clean laundry ready and waiting for me on the bed, and on with the television. They were showing *The Big Lebowski*, in English, and I knew at once that the gods were smiling on me. I angled the TV so as I could watch the movie from the bath, and that's where I stayed, right up until the closing credits had rolled across the screen.

&#8450;&#7439;

## BUTCH, SUNDANCE AND SABATINI TOO

Some people do the nicest things. One of the waiters in the hotels dining room had evidently overheard a comment I'd made some days earlier to one of the Israeli guys about my favourite breakfast food. I believe I'd mentioned something to that effect when discussing the paucity of breakfasts on Kibbutz Amiad, where the culinary options, I seem to recall, were olives or nothing, which only added to my yearning for toast and Marmite.

This morning, as I took my seat at the table by the window, two waiters emerged from the kitchen in convoy, each with a silver platter. They lifted the lids with all the drama they could muster to reveal, respectively, piping hot toast, burned at the edges - they must heard that too - and a brand new pot of Marmite, which heaven only knows must be as rare a commodity on a La Paz supermarket shelf as gold dust.

I was touched, I was thrilled, I was ravenous, and after downing a barge-load of the brown stuff I bade a fond farewell to the staff at the El Rey Palace - I wish I'd had something to leave them other than what little remained of the Marmite - and headed out to the central bus station for the drive to Oruro, and thereafter the long, lazy train-ride to Uyuni.

The bus ride was surprisingly comfortable, a welcome, if terminally uninspiring, antedote to the Yungas ride. There's nothing much wrong with this stretch of the Southern Altiplano, except how staggeringly little it varies in the three hours it takes from La Paz to Oruro. It's flat, it's featureless, it's just like The Fens, and you long for something, anything - say a field mouse crossing the road, or a sudden gust of wind blowing the dust in the other direction - to add a little drama to the proceedings.

Alas not. All that was left was to recline my seat, don my specs, and get to grips with the latest Howard Jacobson, who writes about dysfunctional relationships with such authority and insight it's hard to believe he didn't grow up in my family.

I also indulged myself in a little map reading. I've always loved poring over maps, ever since I was a kid and wanted to run away from home, and my Bolivia map was particularly good and detailed, right down to the last contour and compass point. Reading the map gave me a real frisson of excitement, especially on seeing that the Salar de Uyuni, the legendary Salt Desert, which was to be the next days adventure, is so close to the border of Chile you can almost picture the Pacific Ocean hugging the horizon just across the skinny cordillera. Little things like that do it for me. Don't ask me why; I just love geographical detail, in all its geographical minutiae.

We rolled into Oruro at lunchtime and I was met off the bus by a local tour guide, an almost unbearably gorgeous Gabriella Sabatina lookalike who called herself Graziella. A burgeoning friendship, I'm bound to admit, seemed a mighty fine prospect, albeit distinctly improbable, given the dual constraints of time and marriage.

Almost all of Oruro's 150,000 inhabitants are of pure Indian heritage and refer to themselves as *quirquinchos*, which translates as armadillos. The reason for such a label remains lost on me. But one thing I do know - the women of Oruro are among the most beautiful I have ever seen, a score and more Graziellas on every avenida, and with barely two hours to kill before the train pulled out for Uyuni I accepted Graziella's gracious offer of a 90-minute whistle-stop walking tour of Oruro, if only to indulge myself in some serious bird-spotting.

As it turns out 90 minutes was about 80 minutes longer than was needed to see Oruro. Firstly it was siesta time in Oruro, and most of the townsfolk, gorgeous women and all, were scuttling back home for the duration. But the real reason is that Oruro enjoys almost zero tourism, and it's not hard to see why. 150,000 residents it may have, but with scarcely a tourist attraction to wave an admission ticket at, the only real reason for arriving in town is to put Milton Keynes into some kind of healthier perspective. If you told me Oruro had been twinned with Stevenage, frankly I'd believe you.

No matter. The main plaza was nice enough. I can always while away an hour in a eucalyptus-shaded garden square, and I did enjoy sharing a walk, a drink, and a freshly baked bag of cookies with Graziella. And any such city that calls itself, as Oruro does, the 'Folkloric Capital of Bolivia' - which is tantamount to Rochdale calling itself 'The Cultural Capital of England' - clearly has a finely-honed sense of self-parody that is to be applauded.

Soon enough it was time to board the train for the 6-hour southerly journey to Uyuni. What a great train - a big, shiny, silver thing with a seemingly endless production line of big, shiny, silver carriages, just like the train in that awful film with Gene Wilder and Richard Pryor, the one where the only good thing in it was the train. And what a nice ride. First class carriage, reclining seat, foot rest, TV and video, wide selection of Bolivian motoring magazines, mostly of the repair-your-broken-down-Toyota variety, and even a half-decent dining car.

On the dot of three we pulled out of Ururo. At five past three a waiter came round bearing boiled sweets. Ten past it was yoghurts, soft drinks and industrial-sized bags of dried fruit; twenty past, bread and biscuits; half past, chocolate éclairs and gooey cake things; twenty-five to, ice cream and wafers; and so it went, cholesterol on wheels.

The first leg of the journey was very fine indeed, as we wended our way along a narrow spit between the flamingo-festooned lakes of Uru Uru and the gloriously named Poopo. So much more alluring, don't you think, than Wastwater and the Welsh Harp. The afternoon sun flooded in through the window and I had a little snooze, before heading down to the dining car for a late lunch. It was full of Israelis, as though they'd be anywhere other than where the food is.

I knew they were Israeli before a word was spoken. You develop an instinct for this sort of thing. Call it a gut feel, call it fraternal empathy. Actually, call it the ubiquitous silver Oakley sun-glasses pushed high up on their heads in that semi-suave, I'm-so-cool kind of a way that post-army Israelis do so well, before spoiling it all by hitting on some poor unsuspecting foreign blonde with the cheapest chat-up line you ever heard, usually starting and ending with the words: "Er...I fuck you, yes?" I picked up a coffee and returned to my seat, and I scarcely looked up from my book for the better part of an hour.

When, eventually, I did peer out the window, the terrain had changed totally and dramatically. It was all salt and lithium, or whatever else might balance the mood swings of the desert. And all the while the sun was throwing off a perfectly dazzling array of colour and shade across an otherwise desolate landscape, magentas and ochres bouncing against the grubby off-white of the desert floor. And all of this offset by the creams and browns of the llamas that were grazing where, it has to be said, there seemed precious little on which to graze. Very strange, very surreal, very Bolivian.

Even weirder, quite spooky in fact, were the ghost towns we passed. One of them, surely, was San Vicente, where Robert LeRoy Parker and Harry Alonzo Longabaugh - better known as Butch Cassidy and the Sundance Kid - met their end back in 1908. I'd like to think so. I've seen the movie more times than I care to remember and it's a nice, romantic notion when you're headed out from oblivion to the middle of nowhere in a setting rich in cinematic fantasy.

In truth there was no way of knowing the names of any of the towns we passed through. They were all unsigned, deathly anonymous, the lands that time forgot. And they looked, every last one of them, as though they'd not been inhabited since...well, since 1908, the only sign of life along the way being a lone mule, the actual one horse in the proverbial one horse town. That, and a lone back-packer who, I would like to believe, was an obsessive movie buff on a mystical quest to find the exact spot where Butch and Sundance had their last, fatal gunfight.

But then, who would live here? All that open space, yes. But it's covered either in sand, salt, or a particularly dense strain of glutinous mud. And the buildings, from what I could see, comprised either a wall, a roof, a window or a door...but never the whole lot, leaving no doubt as to where the Hole In The Wall Gang got their name.

We trundled on along our southerly way, darkness descending almost imperceptibly. Day becomes night in minutes in these parts; the Southern Altiplano is famous for it. You blink, you miss it. With the bawdy Mr. Jacobson on my lap for the next couple of hours, time passed quickly and agreeably, and in the twinkling of an eye we had pulled into Uyuni and hitched up our wagon on the dot of nine.

That was close on twelve hours on the road. Never mind how relaxing the journey was; dawn-to-dusk hiking, even on wheels, is pretty damn tiring in anyone's language. So imagine my delight at being met off the train by a chirpy young guide called Dietmar, who whisked me with a smile and a song to a tumbledown little hacienda called the Hosteria La Magia.

This was something of a departure from what I had originally planned, which was two nights at the Palacio de Sal, though the reason, I'm bound to admit, was more than compelling. For that particular hostelry, which enjoys an apparently idyllic setting by the salt lake, was that very morning flooded out by the salt lake. This left me no choice. The Magia it was. More basic than Michael Barrymore's swimming skills, but a bed's a bed, and when you're cream-crackered from a long day on the road you take what you can get.

I pushed open the door to my room and fell headlong into a Marx Brothers movie. You remember that broom cupboard of a cabin Groucho was given on the liner in *A Night At The Opera*, the one half of Hollywood came tumbling out of when

## PLACES BEGINNING WITH 'B'

Margaret Dumont opened the door? My broom cupboard was smaller. A single bed and absolutely nowhere - neither a cupboard nor a chair nor one single, solitary wire coat hanger - to hang my clothes or lay down a book or two. A window would have been nice too. They say there are no telephone boxes in Uyuni. Pity. Had I found one I'd have signed a lease there and then and moved on in, just for that feeling of space.

I didn't hang around to sample the joys of claustrophobia. Instead I headed into town for a late-night nosh and a taste of Uyuni. This is the upside of arriving somewhere after dark. It's one part instinct, nine parts guesswork as to what the place is like, which only whets the appetite for the dawning of the next day.

My instinct in this case said pure Wild West, a Dodge City for the southern hemisphere or was I just being influenced by my own vivid imagination and all those tales of Butch and Sundance holing up in Bolivia's south-west? OK, it's up top of a high plateau at 12,000 feet, night temperatures drop to a miserly 20 below, and there's no-one around, not that I could see anyway, called Doc Halliday, Dances With Latkes or Sitting Shiva. But I felt the spirit of Butch and The Kid all around me, and if I'd had a pistol in my holster and an Oscar on my mantelpiece, I'd have crouched with the best of them in a bullet-riddled doorway to a bullet-riddled bank. Ah, the romance.

☙

## A NIGHT AT THE OPRAH

Hosteria La Magia inhabits, it seems to me, a different stratosphere to anywhere I've ever stayed before, tents and open air excepted. The broom cupboard bedroom I could live with, even without a cupboard, a chair, a hanger or a window. So long as it had a light switch and a radiator I'd have been happy enough, ecstatic even. But no. There was no light, no heating, nothing much at all really to suggest I hadn't lost my way round the back of the building, opened a door, and stumbled into the cold store. The place was freezing. You notice these things when you're pushing fifty and your blood has the skimpily thin consistency of the water from which you emerged. Here, then, is a list of what lay on, under and around me in bed last night in a pathetic, and ultimately futile, attempt at keeping warm:

Item 1: A sheet, origins unknown, rice paper a distinct possibility
Item 2: 2 blankets, llama wool possibly, more likely a bulimic duck
Item 3: One eiderdown, flimsy
Item 4: Thermal Socks, 2 pairs
Item 5: Thermal leggings, 1 pair
Item 6: Thermal sweater, just the one
Item 7: Thermal hat, polartec lining
Item 8: 3 T-shirts from various ancient rock gigs, one of them, ironically, The Electric Light Orchestra
Item 9: 1 Polartec jacket draped seductively, if ineffectively, around my upper half. AND STILL I WAS COLD!

I'd like to say the day began with a piping hot shower and a bath sheet warmed on a heated towel rail - but hey, who am I kidding? Instead I stripped off a few layers, doused myself in ice cold water, and made straight for the breakfast room in search of a bowl of steaming porridge and a fluffy omelette. Along the way I spotted an ancient paraffin heater, which I decided to kick-start into what might pass for action. It fell over and died.

I took my place at the breakfast table and found myself squatting next to a sixty-something Jewish couple from Great Neck, or Yonkers, or some such other daftly-named New York suburb. (Say what you will about Hendon, at least it *sounds* sensible). My cup of distempered mucus dispatched - I'd call it coffee, but I'm aware of the laws governing misrepresentation - I headed out with Dietmar and our dodgy Toyota on our journey to the back of beyond.

Never before did I see so much nothingness as on that incredible journey. The remoteness was total, like driving from Utah to Wyoming via Siberia and the Yukon. We drove along the salt lakes of the Daniel Campos province. That's right - driving on lakes. A bed of brilliant white hexagonal salt tiles, the azure of the Altiplano sky and the distant peaks of the Chilean Andes reflected with crystal clarity in the six-inch layer of water that covers the whole expanse of this saline desert as it stretches a hundred miles beyond the horizon.

The sun dazed and dazzled as we fetched up a couple of hours later at Colchani, a primitive confection of sheds and shacks that grandly calls itself a processing plant. This is where the billions of tons of salt that have been hacked away with pick and shovel are turned into table salt and packaged for export. The whole thing is done manually, in mud-roofed huts under straw roofs and with naked flames instead of electricity, which leans a little heavily, wouldn't you say, on the indulgence of the fire officers of the Daniel Campos Province.

We continued along the salt lake, surrounded by more than enough conical pillars of salt to suggest this might just be the place where that wily old reprobate Lot

turned nasty on his wife and transformed her into one half of a condiment set. And the further we drove, the more wild and desolate our surroundings became, and with it the possibility, the very real possibility, that we were soon to lose all touch with civilization. What we needed was an oasis, a mirage that we could see, touch and enter with our own senses.

We found one. For this leg of the drive took us to our base for the night, the fabled and seriously conceptual Salt Hotel, a drop dead contender for entry into the Independent on Sunday's *Top Ten Most Exotic Honeymoon Hideaways*, and yes, the one concession to civilization and honeymooning for many a long mile.

The hotel stands in splendid isolation in the middle of the lake and is built entirely from hulking great slabs of salt, all of it, except for a bizarre conical straw roof that makes the whole place look somehow like an albino Worzel Gummidge with windows. The salt theme continues inside. Salt walls, salt floors, salt tables, salt chairs, salt beds. There's even a pool table made of salt, with salt cues and salt pockets and a length of green baize that, who knows, may just be made of salt. Just don't ask for salt with your food. There isn't any. They used it all in the building. If you want salt on your latkes you'll have to lick the table.

I dropped off my stuff and went back to the dodgy Toyota to continue our drive out to the middle - the very, *very* middle - of the salt lakes, in essence the middle of nowhere, the Centre of the Earth of which Jules Verne might have written, given a bigger budget and a lesser sense of geography. We were off to Isla Incahuasi.

We were squishing our way through the water when, halfway across, Dietmar and I decided to clamber up and ride on the roof rack, leaving our driver alone and bereft of the moral support that this ageing, ailing machine evidently craved. Vehicles have feelings too, you know, and sure enough it wasn't long before the Toyota juddered and shuddered to a spluttery and deeply depressive halt.

Thereafter it broke down so often it needed not so much a mechanic as a therapist. You could time the breakdowns like contractions, every twenty minutes, preceded by much coughing and choking, making the kind of noises normally associated with contestants on *Who Wants To Be a Millionaire*. This was a sad, deeply unhappy vehicle. Put it on TV and it would have confessed it's many sins to Oprah Winfrey..

So...here's the thing. We're in the middle of the desert, a very salty, very wet, and extremely unforgiving desert, variously referred to, depending on prevailing weather conditions, as salt desert, salt flat, salt plains, or salt lake. There are no road markings, no road signs, *no road*, no cat's eyes, no lighting or illumination of any kind, beyond what nature provides...nothing, in fact, to suggest that the sum total of inhabitants on this planet numbered any more than the three of us and a vehicle that was fast developing all the characteristics of a recently bereaved pensioner who has all but lost the will to live.

Let's face it - we were up a certain place without a certain implement, surrounded by enough salt and water to cater a Passover Seder. What to do? Well, after much huffing and puffing, and the ingenious use of chewing gum, boot laces, sweet wrappers, snotty hankies, and discarded hosiery (mostly Dietmar's, but that's another story), we patched up some of the faulty bits under the bonnet and gave the cruiser a wee bit more life than it deserved. This may sound harsh, but a desert-bound vehicle that carries nothing so rudimentary as a tool kit deserves to die.

And with that we reached Isla Incahasi without too much further mishap, albeit at a snail's pace. The vision that was set before me was one I shall never forget, an other-worldly natural paradise of soaring, jagged pinnacles and gigantic 30 foot cacti rising to a crescendo at the island's highest point.

The summit itself looks out across the salt deposits all the way to the Chilean Andes, the clouds and volcanoes reflected with such clarity in the flat white sea of salt tiles, you could stand on your head and the whole thing would look exactly the same upside down. The salt tiles really do provide a perfect mirror for anything above or beyond.

We lunched al fresco - on a desert island there is only al fresco - squatting gingerly between the pine needles and spiky cacti, while tiny little voles scurried around our feet in search of discarded crisps and breadcrumbs. The sun beat down on our heads with a Biblical fury, and if God himself had popped out from behind a bush, burning or otherwise, I for one would not have been the least bit surprised. This was heaven on Earth.

It seemed a pity to have to leave the island - cynics rarely get the chance to meet their maker - but

Dietmar was keen to nail the return journey inside three hours and catch the sunset from the hotel's salt patio. Fat chance. The car just wouldn't stop breaking down, as a result of which the sun set itself to the cacophonous sound of choking carburettors, nauseous head gaskets, and cursing Bolivians.

Twelve times we ground to a halt on that journey and twelve times we waited heaven knows how long for the engine to cool down, re-engage and start up...like anything needs to cool down in sub-zero temperatures. By now the sky was pitch black and a long cold night on the tiles loomed large.

The Toyota, to be brutally honest, was a crock of shell-shocked shit. No tool kit, no rescue kit, no masking tape, no gaffer tape, no red triangle, no torch, no spare wheel, no walkie-talkie, no two-way radio, no mobile phone, no flashing lantern, and definitely no semaphore - we'd already used the snotty hankie, so that was right out. In fact, nothing at all that might reasonably be called means-of-communication. We were alone in the world, in the very heartland of a place called Nowhere, in the freezing, freezing cold, four boiled sweets between us, and our hopes of making it through the night and not winding up cryogenically frozen rapidly diminishing to nothing. If we'd lunched in heaven, I'd hate to say where we were having our afters.

Well, I could bang on about the paucity of equipment around these parts, but suffice to say it took me of all people, feckless old me, to save the day. It wasn't anything so dramatic, really. I was rummaging between the layers of raffia matting loosely masquerading as floor carpet, foraging for more boiled sweets as it happens, when I unearthed the tiniest, flimsiest torch you ever saw. It had, I estimated, no more than fifteen minutes of life left in its fading battery, and I it was who sat on the roof in all my square-jawed, super hero splendour, shivering my bollocks off and flashing the little torch in what I could only guess might possibly be the right direction.

It was. Fifteen minutes and an all-but-dead battery later, and eleven hours after leaving Isla Incahuasi, we were rescued, baled out by a much sleeker, way more glossy Toyota - I'm still not sure whether it's the torch or my halo the driver spotted - and returned to the bosom of the salt world.

We reached the hotel fully three hours into the next day, the mercury struggling to acknowledge the twenty below mark, and I made for where it was at least ten degrees more welcoming. My bed. I emptied my backpack of all my clothes, put them all on, and shivered myself to sleep.

ℭℨ

## THERE AIN'T NO STRUMPETS IN THE OLD TESTAMENT

OK, tell me I'm stupid. I'd endured the kind of night - and this is indoors, remember, not Everest Base Camp - that turns your goolies to ice, and sleep, it has to be said, had not exactly been something I'd fully gotten to grips with the previous few hours. And yet, I was up and about before six. There's a reason for this - the sunrise, which I so wanted to see and which is said around these parts to be nothing short of magical. And so it was.

Dawn's first chorus brought the most wonderful, lustrous sky bursting forth to spread its reds, blues and yellows like a celestial duvet right across the submerged hexagons of desert salt, and in one spellbinding flash of beauty all of yesterday's shenanigans with dodgy motors were consigned to history. I can think of no more bewitching place to be than the Salar de Uyuni at the breaking of a new day. If ever I were looking for a new visualisation to replace Leanne and the massed ranks of REM, this was it.

My first, and biggest, decision of the day was taken out of my hands by a very nice German couple. The matter in hand was how to get to Potosi, because I sure as hell wasn't about to saddle a villainous old Toyota which, frankly, I wouldn't trust even to have its tailgate opened without collapsing in an irredeemable heap of twisted metal and soggy sweet wrappers. If this were a getaway car, I wouldn't back it to get away from a push-bike.

The German couple, to whom news of my nocturnal misadventures had already spread like the stuff of legend, leapt into the fray and offered to let me share their private taxi to Potosi. The bonus here, aside from the comfort and relative speed of a fully functioning vehicle, is that they were heading off out with their guide at 7.30. This was fully four hours before my bus was due to leave Uyuni. Plus it's four hours by taxi, as compared to nine by bus, which means I'd hit Potosi in time for lunch rather than supper. I accepted their offer with gleeful gratitude and hopped on board for Potosi.

Potosi is pretty damn high up the mountain. In fact, at 13,500 feet it's the highest city on Earth, and that's official. We were spirited there by means of a smooth old Mercedes, across all manner of terrain, from the salt lakes that led back to Uyuni, to the open prairies of Bolivia's desolate Wild West, which was so wild, so desolate, we encountered scarcely another vehicle or living soul for the better part of two hours. This was scrubby wasteland at its scrubbiest and most wasted.

Bolivia has a real genius for place names, the equal of anywhere in England, and God knows our place names are daft enough. Residents of Pratts Bottom and the little known west country hamlet of Fondle-Me-Softly would doubtless fight the English corner on this one. But remember, it's only a few days since I skirted the shores of lakes Uru Uru and Poopo Poopo.

I mention this because the first settlement we encountered on the road to Potosi - and I use the word settlement because hamlet would be overstating the case, while village would be a gross exaggeration of the highest water - was called Tica Tica, a ragbag affiliation of derelict buildings that should long ago have been pensioned off and reduced to rubble, though there was little about the place to suggest that the process had not already begun.

And here's the amazing thing. People live here. They may have potting sheds for living rooms, craters for toilets, and quite possibly jumpers for goalposts, but to the folk out here this is home, and I regard it as nothing short of a privilege each time I discover on my travels such stark and, in a curious kind of way, thrilling contrast to the terminally bland suburbs of the first world. I'm not sure I'd hack it for too long without a full set of outside walls, but I'd take comfort, for a short while at least, from the magnificence of my surroundings, the crimson mountains, the cactus-filled canyons, and the grazing alpaca and vicuna.

This vista continued for a while, the rock formations getting weirder and wackier, at times like a hybrid of the huge monolithic pillars of Timna Park down in the Negev and the humanoid projections and promontories of Mount Rushmore. This was one hell of a place. Very strange, very special and, I was fast coming to realise, very Bolivian.

We rolled into Potosi on the dot of one, to find what I can only describe as a quite immense military presence. Roads were blocked off, rifles were slung menacingly and meaningfully over scores of uniformed shoulders, and if anarchy hadn't already broken out, it sure as heck looked like it was about to.

Evidently, and quite inadvertently, we had arrived at the exact same moment as the entire city was about to go on strike. Let me repeat that...*the entire city was going on strike*. The butcher, the baker, the candle-stick maker, and, I have no doubt, every last kindergarten kid too. Everyone, it seems, was railing against the city's public-serving drivers, who were themselves amassing on the steps of the city's municipal centre to begin a week-long sit-in. In other words, a protest against a protest.

No-one that I asked seemed to have the faintest idea what the drivers were protesting against. Not that it mattered. This is Bolivia after all, and in Bolivia no-one needs anything quite so old-fashioned as a reason in order to stage a strike, protest, sit-in or occupation.

Of course, there *was* a reason, as I was soon to find out, for not even in South America would quite so many as 75,000 working stiffs down tools and take themselves off the payroll unless it really mattered. And the reason, so I was told by a local café owner who was making a killing selling cups of soup to the assembled masses, was that the drivers had themselves fallen foul of an industrial action by the manufacturers of spare car parts, without which no Bolivian vehicle can function for much longer than a day-and-a-half. In other words, a protest against a protest *against* a protest.

The term 'public-serving drivers' covers bus drivers, coach drivers, train drivers and taxi drivers...and that includes private taxi drivers...and with me needing to get to Sucre tomorrow, you can see how this might present something of a problem, not least as from Sucre I was to catch a flight the following day down to Santa Cruz, and then on to Rio. What to do?

The solution was simple, largely because there *was* only one solution. Get the guide who brought me in to town to pull every string in his quiver, and get me the hell out of town and down to Sucre. This he achieved with commendable efficiency. Within ten minutes he'd phoned through to Sucre and booked me into the town's newest, and apparently poshest, hotel, plus a private taxi to get me there...a perfectly conceived plan that would work a treat just so long as the taxi pissed off out of Potosi before the official start of the drivers' strike at 1.30.

We left town at 1.28.

I guess I was slightly regretful not to have got to see Potosi's famous old silver mines. But to all downsides, an upside, in this case the chance to spend even more time in what many regard as the finest city in all of Bolivia, and at barely a 2-hour taxi ride away, I'd find out soon enough the truth of such claims.

The drive to Sucre passed pleasantly enough, although by now I'd have gladly traded all the mountain roads in South America for a hot bath, a steaming bowl of pasta with basil pesto and sun-dried tomatoes, and a frothy great vat of bubbling cappuccino. And if, per chance, they could all be administered by a fulsome young wench called Lilith, Delilah or Hephzibah, so much the better. I reckon I deserved it.

Well, what can I tell you? No strumpet with an Old Testament name, to be sure. But everything else I wanted, I got. The Hotel Independence was splendid, a real gem. Just off the main plaza, clean, comfy and warm, with oodles of hot water in the tub, plus a Sony widescreen TV in my room that had the great good foresight to be showing two of my very favourite films - *Still Crazy* and *This Is Spinal Tap* - back to back. I really couldn't say for sure if God exists, but if he does he certainly spent a lot longer than any of us mere mortals in the Seventies, getting stoned and soaking up all that sex, drugs and rock-and-roll excess.

Refreshed, refurbished, and with heavy metal in my heart, I hopped the few yards to the piazza, found myself a cosy little trattoria adorned with Italian football memorabilia, and had myself that bowl of pasta and bubbling cappuccino I'd so coveted these past hours. The owner of the restaurant was a one time Genoese shipyard worker, long domiciled in Bolivia, and now a highly entrepreneurial bigwig in the Italian food business in this neck of the woods.

His name was Gianluca, and from the generous size of his girth - which, from a distance of, say, ten metres could be easily mistaken for the Equator - I'd say he never once served a meal without first sampling a very large ladleful himself. Gianluca and I hit it off straight away. With a shared passion for the Italian sweeper system and the team of '94 that really should have won the World Cup, our immediate friendship was never in any serious doubt, and I was not in the least surprised when he offered to show me the sights of Sucre the following morning.

Gianluca's cooking was absolutely splendid, as was his company, and when, finally, I rolled back to the hotel it was with a warm tummy and not a thermal in sight that I sunk down under the duvet on my queen-sized bed, slept the deep, heavy sleep of the extremely well fed, and dreamed the dreams of a middle-aged man in a state of rare contentment.

## NOW I KNOW WHAT JOE PESCI FEELS LIKE

I was cajoled, coerced, and finally bullied from my slumbers barely a second or two after the hour hand on my watch struck six. I had no choice in the matter. It's mandatory around these parts. There's no law about it, not so far as I know. No Act of Parliament, no statutory declaration, nothing like that. Just pealing church bells from next door the hotel, squealing children of the extremely pre-pubescent variety across the road to the hotel - and why weren't they out shining shoes, you might ask - and an extremely menopausal cockerel who seemed to have lost his way somewhat and wound up, I can only conclude from the severity of the noise, in the adjacent room. In short, I was Joe Pesci in *My Cousin Vinny*, woken, whether I liked it or not, by a conspiracy of noise at an unearthly hour.

No matter. The sun defied the earliness of the hour and fairly streamed in to my room without shame or pity. Frankly that's all the incentive I needed to drag myself out of bed and on to the street. Brilliant sunshine rouses me every time and no mistake. Showered, dressed and breakfasted I stepped outside to take the dawn air only to make a startling, and hugely welcome, discovery.

There, between hotel and church, was a gym. Goodness me, but this was La Paz revisited. I couldn't believe my luck. I went back to my room, dug out my kit, and popped next door, first customer of the day, for a rummage through the antiquated, but perfectly serviceable, weights, before showering, changing, and meeting up with Gianluca for my informal city tour.

I couldn't help noticing he had a car with him. He couldn't help noticing my stated preference to leg it. To me, a car is no way to see a city. You need to be on your feet to get a real feel for the place, and never mind how nose-bleedingly steep that place is...and the streets of Sucre are nothing if not steep, reminiscent in every last screaming sinew and rebellious tendon of Lisbon's Alfama district.

We took in all there was on the colonial trail. Cathedral, Supreme Court, street market, book fair, handicraft and tapestry museums, the customary statue to Simon Bolivar, in fact several statues to Simon Bolivar, whose ubiquity is matched only by his vanity. In every sense a whistle stop tour, giving little time to any one sight, but more than enough overview to paint the prettiest of pictures of this hugely appealing town.

The high point - and that's high point in all senses - is Le Recoleta, an idyllic little piazza at the top of the Calle Polanco with a cool, cloistered convent in one corner, a pergola-covered terrace in the other, and an expansive view across the whole of Sucre from under the fabulous Cedro Milenario, the huge ancient cedar whose branches cast filtered sunlight across the square.

The panorama that unfolded was little short of breathtaking, and one that, in some ways, owes much to the local piece of bureaucracy that insists all buildings within the central core of the city are either whitewashed or painted white. And it's a bureaucracy too, though they would call it civic pride, that has the locals trying valiantly to convince themselves that Sucre is still Bolivia's capital city, as indeed it once was. Judicially speaking it still is. But if the Supreme Court still convenes in Sucre, it's La Paz that has long usurped the real governmental power in Bolivia.

Sucre, though, is every bit as alluring a city as La Paz, and where Bolivia's de facto capital has on its outskirts the beguiling red canyons of Moon Valley, Sucre is fringed to the south by the brilliant green and violet hillsides of the Crater de Maragua.

But it's the colonial sea of white villas and palazzos with their terracotta roofs that sets Sucre apart, and as I stood under the spreading cedar tree gazing out over this halcyon scene, it suddenly dawned on me: this could be Andalucia. Sucre is a facsimile in every last sense of the *pueblos blancos* of Southern Spain. My camera whirred and whirled into overdrive, and with each photograph taken came an even more stunning view to record for posterity. Bolivians refer to Sucre as *The White City* of the Americas. I guess they've never been to Shepherd's Bush.

My walking tour with Gianluca passed pleasantly enough, and when lunchtime came I could see no good reason to turn down his offer of a complimentary pizza and a slab or two of exquisitely home-made tiramisu. Once more I waddled out of his establishment with a quite extraordinary amount of food inside me before treating my trusty old boots to a spit and polish on the main piazza.

I wasn't too sure what to do next, so I wandered the narrow lanes between the Plaza 25 de Mayo and the Avenida Hernando Siles and found myself inexorably drawn to the local barber shop, which - and you have only to see a photograph of me to understand why - is as unlikely as the Chief Rabbi's fingers walking through Yellow Pages for the nearest Macdonalds.

This is no self-referential irony on my part. I really wanted to see the barber shop, for the barber shop in question was the fabled and nostalgically retro Soliz Barber Shop, and I was keen to see the handiwork, the 1920s silent movie star haircuts, of the legendary Jaime Soliz, Sucre's answer to Vidal Sassoon.

I can't say I'd ever before given serious consideration, or *any* consideration, to watching people having their hair cut or whiskers shaved for my own personal amusement. But such is the artistry of Jaime Soliz, and the intensity with which he wields his razors, it was like witnessing the reincarnation of Pablo Picasso, Sweeney Todd, and any number of Hollywood make-up artists in one fell swoop.

I was absolutely spellbound by this minor exhibition of crimping - I'd love to see highlights of the highlights one day - and although my Spanish is nothing to write home about, I do know the words *senor*, *algo*, and *fin de semana*, and I can therefore report that even in this wild south-west corner of the world, Sir can still be offered something for the weekend.

I whiled away what remained of the afternoon sitting out in the piazza under the sun, bargaining with the local vendors for bits of cloth I'd never use, love-beads I'd

never wear, and shoe-shines I no longer needed. I did buy myself a new Parker pen at the local stationery store, having mislaid my favourite old silver version I know not where. This may seem like an absurdly minor piece of detail to record in a journal, but these things are important to a writer, and losing a pen that had written up my notes from Peru to Ecuador, Costa Rica to Belize, Kilimanjaro to the Galapagos Islands, and all stations between and beyond, whilst not enough to bring down governments, is certainly a bit of a bummer. Still, I had a plane to catch.

The early evening flight to Santa Cruz took all of 32 minutes, making it the shortest hop I'd made, aviation-wise, since flying from Leavesden Airstrip to Elstree Aerodrome many years ago. Time enough, I thought, to run in my new Parker, be it on my journal or on conquering the *News of the World Bumper Quiz Book,* which for some reason is a big hit in stationery shops in Sucre.

I thought wrong. I'd just buckled myself in, ravenously clawing away at the wrapper of a mammoth two-pound bar of Dairy Milk, when the whole plane jerked, jolted and shuddered in a way that suggested one of two things. Either the plane, or at least some small component therein, was manufactured by Toyota, or if not by Toyota per se, then by someone whose primary training was in the Japanese automotive industry...or my old friend Leanne was on board.

"Hey Buddy. D'you wanna do a line with me, squeeze into a cubicle and..."
"Hi Leanne".

She leaned forward from the seat - *seats* - behind and practically drowned me with what I now realise was a kiss. A bath towel would be scarcely sufficient to wipe the drench off my neck. I'd learned in Copacabana to admire Leanne's peculiar brand of smooth talk and verbal foreplay. I'm not sure about the "squeeze into a cubicle" bit, though. Who's she kidding? This girl couldn't squeeze into a supermarket. Mind you, so far as the cocaine bit goes, I didn't doubt her for one moment. Trafficking the stuff in South America is a pretty dumb thing to do. But this girl has got so much bulk, secreting the stuff should present no problem whatsoever. There are parts of her body no man would ever dare go, with or without a sniffer dog, and pity the poor sap who tries.

"Did I tell you about the time I helped nurse Che Guevera through his malnutrition in La Higuera back in '67?" she asked. "Of course, he died soon after, but not before we..."
"Leanne", I said, "please don't tell me this; let me believe he died a hero's death...please". And with that I pulled out a deck of cards, proposed a hand or two of poker, and relieved Leanne of $30 in about as many minutes.

We touched down in Santa Cruz just before six. At least, I touched, she plummeted. Big girl, Leanne. Very big girl. With the benefit of hindsight I rather wish I'd had Leanne for company in Santa Cruz. But alas not. I was sticking around town for a day or so, while she was moving straight on out to the Amazon jungle, doubtless to advance the cause of over-eating among the stick-thin missionaries of the Eastern Lowlands.

My guide was there to meet and greet me, by 6.30 I was checking in at the Royal Lodge Hotel in what my esteemed son Gideon might describe as a big fat suite, and as the clock struck 6.45 I was checking out the unexpectedly modern gym next door. I don't usually use the gym twice in the one day - I'm not *that* obsessive - but when opportunities present themselves in such unlikely fashion, and when I've been feeling a tad more slothful than I've been used to, it's more than I can do to turn them down.

The hotel was well away from the city centre. So, with another workout done and dusted I cabbed it downtown to the Plaza 24 de Septembre and found myself all at once consumed with déjà vu. It was the self same piazza as the one I'd just left behind in Sucre, right down to the criss-cross paths that run diagonally though the square, the overhanging palm trees, cathedral tucked up in one corner, and Senor Bolivar lording it over the whole damn thing from his vantage point on a plinth high above the park benches.

And then it occurred to me - this is what *every* piazza in Bolivia looks like. In fact, it's what every piazza in all of South America looks like. They really are utterly interchangeable, the only variation I know being Bolivar's deferring to Pele in Rio de Janeiro...and quite right too.

What really marked this piazza as thoroughly unique, though, was its complete absence of human beings. To put it bluntly, it was dead. Supper time and not a soul in sight. And to compound the sad, sorry debunking of all that I'd come to expect of South American piazzas, the only bar of any kind to grace the perimeter of the square rejoiced in the singularly depressing name of The Irish Pub. How sad is that?

And before you say "what about Cuzco?", let me remind you that at least the Cross Keys Pub in that very wonderful Peruvian city shows wall-to-wall Manchester United to wall-to-wall trekkers just back from hiking the Inca Trail. Plus they do a mean toast and Marmite, and Gil, who spins the discs - or he did when I was last there - re-stocks the thing with whatever his more discerning, or in my case opiniated, punters happen to bring with them to the bar, in my case a backpackful of Talking Heads and Clash CDs, which made Christmas Eve 1998 last a day or two longer than anyone expected.

Alas, no such jollity and japery in Santa Cruz. Nothing to do, in fact, but head back to the hotel for a banana split, another vat of cappuccino, and an early night with Doris Day and Rock Hudson dubbed in Spanish. Such a disappointment.

CB

## WHEN MEN GET BORED THEY MAKE LISTS

I leapt from my bed with the clarion call of positivity ringing in my ears. I passed on breakfast and headed instead straight for the centre of town to see if it might be better by day. It wasn't. If anything it was worse, markedly so. It was 9.30, by which time any city worth its salt should be up and running and seriously kicking sand in a thousand-and-one faces. Not Santa Cruz.

The first thing I noticed was the inordinate number of car showrooms on the way into town. Every other plate glass window was showing off one or other brand of Japanese car. They were all there, all the usual suspects. Toyota, Mazda, Mitsubishi, Honda, Lexus, Nexus, Plexus. It was like the Colindale end of the Edgware Road, another thoroughfare awash in Japanese car showrooms, except this being Bolivia the cars had probably next to no chance of making it over the threshold and onto the street without first disintegrating in an oily puddle of death.

The next thing I noticed was people, the singular lack of. I don't understand it. If Santa Cruz really is home to a million-and-a-half souls, then where the hell are they? Actually, with the highest number, pro rata, of 12-bedroom homes on the face of the Earth, the question rather answers itself. The good folk of Santa Cruz, it seems, can't find their way out of their houses. Right now there's probably some poor senorita who went to open her front door some time last year, got lost along the way, and is still struggling to disentangle herself from the light pulley in the downstairs toilet.

And with an even higher ratio of Nazis-on-the-run - for Bolivia has long given succour to the dregs of the planet - Santa Cruz is clearly a place where a low profile is something of a pre-requisite. So strong is the Germanic presence in this corner of the southern hemisphere, it's sometimes a struggle to find a Suarez and a de la Cruz in among the Hallers and the Himmlers in the local Yellow Pages.

And animals. Where are the animals? I had heard that the main piazza at Santa Cruz was famed for its resident population of three-toed sloths who, it is said, will willingly leap out of their trees and on to the park benches at the dangling of a ripened banana. Sloths? Never mind sloths. I never glimpsed so much as a sparrow. The whole thing, I have to say, had me pining for…well…almost anywhere else, really.

Part of the problem, I'm bound to admit, is that Santa Cruz is a flat lowlands city, in stark contrast to all those hilly conurbations I've grown so accustomed to in Latin America. As such Santa Cruz really does enjoy not one view, one vista, one drop dead panorama worth the entry fee. It is also irredeemably bland and unforgivably boring. If it were a car you'd call it a Skoda; if it were a person you'd call it Gwyneth Paltrow; if it were in England you'd call it Watford.

The city has no soul and a heartbeat so faint you need to press your ear to the sidewalk to hear it ticking. La Paz might be twice the size of Santa Cruz, but it has way more intimacy and infinitely more blood coursing through its veins. So too Sucre, Coroico and Copacabana, all of which are blessed with that warm backpacking vibe that makes even the most faraway place seem like a home away from home. Santa Cruz, spiritually speaking, is redundant.

Eventually - and I had to wander fully eight blocks from the piazza - I found something approximating, albeit in the loosest way possible, to a café. It was dreadful. Drab, dreary and dismal. Take away the coffee - and I rather wish they had - and it could have been a morgue. It was 10.15 and I do believe I was their first customer of the day. I'd like to have aided their cause by ordering something more than a lone and desultory coffee, but I was on a roll, insofar as I'd found somewhere that was open, and I was keen to move on and find café number two down here in the happening quarter.

Well, by 10.30 things were beginning to look up in Santa Cruz. In fact, by 10.30 hordes of people were looking up in Santa Cruz, specifically on the Plaza 24 de Septembre. The reason? Well, wouldn't you know it, the sloths were in town, and so were the humans, who at last had woken up, smelled the coffee - to say nothing of the sloth shit - and realised that life really is worth living after all.

So there we were, scores of us on sloth-watch, cameras at the ready, waiting eagerly for showtime in the heart of the soporific city. And the show didn't disappoint. A moment or two's theatrical silence, an imaginary drum roll, and then…it hove into view. A fluffy great three-toed sloth, so bizzarely assembled by nature it really was impossible to tell its head from its arse. It was quite the strangest looking creature I ever saw - oddly reminiscent of Reg Presley from The Troggs - and there it was, dangling from a branch just a foot or two above my head.

I've seen some strange looking creatures in my time. The manatees in the Gulf of Mexico come to mind, so too Julia Roberts, who I've always thought of as oddly manatee-like, what with those oceanic lips and barn-sized nostrils. But this one took the biscuit. Actually it *did* take the biscuit, literally. I had a bag of cookies, the ones left over from Oruro, in my day-pack and it was only when the sloth fed from my hand that its mouth, its bum, and a crack in the park bench were at last distinguishable from one another. Suddenly I was pleased to be in Santa Cruz. In fact, so imbued was I with the joys of Santa Cruzean life, I sauntered across the square, up a flight of stairs, and straight into the Irish Pub.

The place was better than I had dared hope. Not much, I'll admit. But it had a nice balcony over the square and a decent enough choice of sandwich and pastry. The real bonus, though, came in the form of a fabulous looking Finnish girl who parked herself at my table, which she didn't have to; I was the only one in there. She engaged me in conversation, convinced I was Fabien Barthez. I did nothing to dispel the notion. I even dropped everything the waiter gave me just to maintain the illusion, though my second espresso I did manage to tip over the bar.

Her name was Tina and she'd just arrived in Bolivia from way down south in Patagonia. She was travelling alone and - get this - she was not averse to falling in with someone else with whom to share the next leg of her travels. I was sorely tempted, I can tell you. But I was due to pull out of the country later that day, plus I'm married and faithful and pure as the driven snow, plus I'd promised myself, in my own mind at least, to Leanne, provided she managed to shed the odd hundred and twenty pounds.

Ah well. I did the noble thing and exhorted her to scout around for another suitable candidate for travel, sex, trekking, climbing, sex, conversation and sex. I realise I was passing up what Basil Fawlty famously once called "having a bit of fun with a Finn" - that's what he told Terry the chef to do before setting fire to the kitchen in one particularly riotous episode - and I've no doubt I could have persuaded my paper to pay for Bolivian overtime on grounds of seriously rampant totty. I'm sure I could have passed it off as some kind of research into inter-personal relations in the southern hemisphere, which means I'd have quite possibly got a 'lifestyle' feature out of it too. But no, I'm a middle-aged bloke with responsibilities, and occasionally - just occasionally - I know when to graciously decline a jelly-on-the-plate offer from a stunning, pouting, extremely blonde and definitely willing Scandinavian girl.

And with that I headed back on to the square to soak up the remains of the day under the baking sun. With little else to do but sit and bask, I got my pen out, shifted once more into Rob Fleming mode, and re-commenced that hysterically sad male activity known as list-making. There follows, then, a roster - pretty comprehensive, and in no particular order - of things seen, done, explored, encountered, endured, climbed, descended, and very nearly fondled these past two weeks in Bolivia, and I do so with full apologies to anything or anyone I might, in my middle-aged forgetfulness, have left out. Here goes...

La Paz - first view
La Paz - general
El Lobos restaurant - general
El Lobos restaurant - Eli and Dorit
Hotel El Rey Palace
Moon Valley
El Alto
Chacaltaya

Hernan the guide
Ruben the guide
Freddie the guide
Graziella the guide
Lake Titicaca
Isla del Sol
Copacabana - general
Copacabana - Cerro Calvario sunset views
Copacabana- Alf@Net Café
Copacabana - Alex-The-Refusenik
Copacabana - Leanne-The-Big-Girl
Choro Trek - general
Choro Trek - Japanese Man
Choro Trek - Rivka, Chuckie, and the Two Teddies
Coroico - general
Coroico - breakfast at Back Stube Konditorri
Oruro
Uyuni
Salt Lake/Desert
Salt Hotel
Isla Incahuasi
Toyotas - those blessed
Toyotas - those cursed
Yungas Road
Sucre
Santa Cruz - general
Santa Cruz - sloths
Santa Cruz - Tina-The-Untouched

Another list successfully negotiated it was time to return to my hotel, and as I did so it occurred to me what might very well be the best thing about Santa Cruz. Leaving. The sloths apart, this place was so stupefyingly comatose it could drive Cliff Richard to fornication, so imagine how pleased I was when my driver turned up 30 minutes early to whisk me to the airport for onward transmission to Rio.

And that was it. Bye Bye Bolivia, hello Brazil, and welcome to a whole new world of possibilities. And as I sat on the plane, I cast my eyes over that last list and wondered how, if only for my own amusement, I might place the sights and the experiences, the places and the people, in some sort of order of merit. I thought a moment, then a moment more, and then it occurred to me...why bother? Comparisons are onerous and only result in endless soul-searching, mind-changing, and a near-constant stream of rhetorical conversations and arguments of the kind that, were anyone to witness such behaviour, would surely end with my long-term committal in an extremely secure state-funded institution.

Now I realise, of course, the inconsistency of that last statement, having dropped many a whopping great hint as to my favourite films, favourite songs, favourite cities, favourite everything, more or less. And if I'm perfectly honest I've long been something of an anorak when it comes to grading pretty much all the meaningless minutiae that helps keep my life ticking over. That is, as I've said, the province of the male species. But I don't want to do that with Bolivia, not just yet anyway.

That said, there is so much over which to enthuse in this weird, wacky and downright wonderful country down in the south-west corner of the world, from that first view of La Paz to the sheer radiance of the Isla del Sol. The Choro trek was a fabulous diversion, and in parts quite extraordinarily beautiful, and I'm sure I'll dream long, hard and often about my ludicrous and never less than eventful drive across the hexagonal salt crystals of the Salar de Uyuni.

I seriously doubt I will ever forget a hair-raising moment of the white knuckle ride up and down the lunatic stretch of potholed chicanery known as the Yungas Road, a highway to be regarded with total awe, both for the most staggering vertical scenery in all of South America, and for the even more staggering number of lives claimed by its every twist and turn. Even Santa Cruz had a certain nobility in its awfulness. It *is* an awful place, and probably damn proud of it. But it's got its sloths and its Irish pub and Japanese cars that seem to work, or at least look as though they work while they sit there in a dozen showroom windows, and for that we are to be truly grateful.

And then there's the people. I had a superb guide in Hernan-who-shall-be-known-as-Ariel, and an even better one in Freddie. Alex-the-Refusenik provided intriguing, if intense, company, and Eli and Dorit gave me with the warmest of heimesche welcomes to the capital city, plus some terrific nosh to keep me fuelled long into the next day.

The Japanese girl on the boat...well...I never even got to first base, but that's her loss, so too the blonde Finnish girl, the big American girl, and the gorgeous Sabatini lookalike who met me off the La Paz-Oruro train.

And finally, of course, there was my all-too-brief sojourn under the sun with The Japanese Man, which made every breathless, sweat-filled moment spent trekking up to his mountain-top retreat worthwhile. He it is, Mr. Tamiji Hanamura de Furio, who, more than anyone, evokes the spirit and the soul of this beguiling and wonderfully rich country. And he it is, more than anyone or any one thing, who gifted me, simply and purely, with moments and memories

that will endure long after I'm done tramping my way around the globe.

I like Bolivia; I like it a lot. It appeals to all my senses. I like the way it looks, the way it sounds, I even like the way it smells. It appeals to me people-wise, music-wise, mountain-wise and lake-wise. But more than anything, it is so blissfully untrodden, so mercifully unspoiled, a haven for fresh discovery and undiscovered pastures. It appeals to my enduring sense of adventure and wonder, this restless nomadic energy allied to a native inquisitiveness that has me regarding myself not just as a wandering Jew, but a *wondering* Jew. For all these reasons, and probably a lot more besides, I just can't get Bolivia out of my system.

Or is it just that I like places beginning with 'B'?

"The specific object of their quest was spiritual. Though they rushed back and forth across the country on the slightest pretext, gathering kicks along the way, their real journey was inward; and if they seemed to trespass most boundaries, legal and moral, it was only in the hope of finding a belief on the other side."

**John Clellond Holmes**
(Writing of **Jack Kerouac's**
characters in *On The Road*)

Across the
Borderline